Other titles in this series

Creation and Evolution
Editor: Derek Burke

Pacifism and War
Editor: Oliver R. Barclay

The Role of Women
Editor: Shirley Lees

In preparation

The Church and its Unity
Politics

Signs, Wonders and Healing

Editor: John Goldingay

Roger Cowley
Tony Dale
Philip H. Hacking
David Huggett
Bill Lees
Peter May

Inter-Varsity Press

INTER-VARSITY PRESS
38 De Montfort Street, Leicester LE1 7GP, England

© Inter-Varsity Press, 1989

Unless otherwise stated, Scripture quotations in this publication are from the Holy Bible, New International Version. Copyright © 1973, 1978, 1984 International Bible Society. Published by Hodder & Stoughton.

First published 1989

British Library Cataloguing in Publication Data

Signs, wonders and healing.—(When
Christians disagree).
1. Christian church. Ministry of healing
I. Goldingay, John   III. Series
265'.82

ISBN 0–85110–796–6

Set in Linotron Sabon 11/12pt
Typeset in Great Britain by
Input Typesetting Ltd, London
Printed in Great Britain at
the University Press, Oxford

Inter-Varsity Press is the book-publishing division of the Universities and Colleges Christian Fellowship (formerly the Inter-Varsity Fellowship), a student movement linking Christian Unions in universities and colleges throughout the United Kingdom and the Republic of Ireland, and a member movement of the International Fellowship of Evangelical Students. For information about local and national activities write to UCCF, 38 De Montfort Street, Leicester LE1 7GP.

Contents

When Christians Disagree

Introducing the series

There are many subjects on which the teaching of the Bible is quite clear. There is a substantial core of Christian theology and ethics that we can confidently proclaim as 'biblical teaching', and those rejecting as well as those accepting the authority of that teaching will agree that such a core exists.

As we try to work out the application of biblical teaching in detail, however, we find areas in which there is no such clear consensus. Christians who are trying equally to be obedient to the teaching of Christ and his carefully instructed apostles come to different conclusions about such subjects as baptism and church government. Some of their differences have been resolved after debate. In Protestant circles, for instance, few would now wish, as some once did, to excommunicate people for advocating birth control. Further discussion has brought substantial agreement. Some questions, however, are not so easily resolved at present; and there is a need for healthy discussion among Christians so that we may arrive, if possible, at an agreed view. If that is not possible, then all of us need to re-examine our view in the light of Scripture and to exchange views, so that we may ensure that our position is not the product of wishful thinking, but is really faithful to the Bible. All of us are influenced in our thinking by our traditions, our education and the general climate of thought of our age. These forces tend to mould our ideas more than we realize, and to make us conform to the fashion of our time, or the traditions in which we were brought up, rather than to revealed truth.

This series of books under the title of *When Christians Disagree* attempts to tackle some of these current debates. Each book has the same fundamental structures. A series of starting 'theses', or a statement of a position (usually excluding the more extreme views on either side), has been sent to the writers. They have been asked to agree or disagree with the 'theses' and to set out a Christian position as they see it. They then have the opportunity to respond to one or more of the other articles written from a different point of view from their own. A short closing summary attempts to clarify the main issues in debate.

All the contributors seek to be ruled by Scripture. Since they do not agree between themselves, the crucial issue is whether one view or another is more consistent with the teaching of the Bible. Some of the problems arise out of the impact upon us of new cultural patterns. These new patterns may or may not be healthy, and that has to be judged by the application of biblical truth which is always health-giving – the good and acceptable and perfect will of God. We are not arguing whether it is easier to believe or do one thing or another in today's world. We are not even asking whether a Christian position seems stupid to the cultured person of today. We are asking whether there are revealed principles that give us at least some guidelines, and perhaps even a clear answer to our problems.

The Bible is authoritative in more than one way: in some areas explicit teaching is given; in other areas the question is left open in such a way that we know there is no universal 'right' answer. Worship provides an example. There are some broad principles; but the Bible seems authoritatively to allow, and perhaps implicitly to encourage, variety in the details of the style and ordering of worship. In such cases we will solve the problem in our own age and culture in obedience to the more basic explicit teachings that we have.

In the areas that this series explores there are some things laid down clearly in Scripture and some that are not. There is, for instance, no biblical instruction as to whether husband or wife should dig the garden; there are no explicit limits drawn to the coercive powers of the state, nor any delineation of the nature of the world before the fall – except that it was very good.

The arguments, therefore, concern first of all whether the Bible does or does not settle certain questions and secondly how far we can go in confident application of those biblical truths that we are given. The demarcation line between these here is important. If we can agree what is clearly taught then all else is in a secondary category, where we know that human opinion is fallible. Some of our discussion is above the line and is therefore most important. Some falls below it and cannot be as vital, even if in practical terms we have to adopt a policy.

OLIVER R. BARCLAY

In memoriam
Roger Cowley

A personal introduction

This is not the volume on charismatic gifts originally envisaged for the series 'When Christians Disagree'. The arrival in Britain of 'power evangelism', emanating from Vineyard Ministries in California and led by John Wimber, gave a new context to discussion of issues to do with charismatic gifts and suggested the need of a book debating the questions with that focus.

My personal acquaintance with 'signs and wonders' dates from 1985, when a team from Vineyard Ministries came to Derby to take a small-scale weekend equivalent to the week-long teaching conferences which had been taking place in several cities in Britain. The leader, Danny Daniels, began to work through part of their standard teaching syllabus, drawing our attention to the nature of Jesus's healing ministry which, he implied, should be a model for ours. In the course of that, however, he told us about his handicapped daughter, who *hadn't* been healed, and about how God used her to minister to other people, not merely despite her disablement but through it. Danny Daniels won me over to take the rest of what he had to say more seriously than I might otherwise have done, by showing me – without intending to, I presume – that he lived in the real world, in a way that I have to.

I met my wife Ann over a boiled egg at a UCCF conference at Swanwick in April 1963, she a medical student, I an ordinand. In April 1965, by which time we were clear that in due course we would marry, I was in London one Sunday to see her. She had developed a limp. While we crossed from one side to the other of Aberdare Gardens in Hampstead as we walked to church in the evening sunshine, she told me without being very histrionic that the obvious diagnosis on the basis of her symptoms was multiple sclerosis, then an unfamiliar illness, now well-known. It involved a malfunctioning of the nervous system which can affect different parts of the body and result in these parts failing to respond properly to messages from the brain. Next day, Ann took herself to the casualty department of her hospital with her symptoms and her diagnosis; they fairly soon confirmed it, admitted her, and put her on a standard treatment, a course of a drug called corticotrophin.

We had found great joy in the love God had given us for each other. Suddenly we found the whole future imperilled. Yet the experience brought to both of us a close sense of the real presence of the loving God in our lives. Further, it raised questions that we had not faced as forcefully before: what meant most to us, having God or having each other? The next Sunday I hitch-hiked back to London to see Ann in hospital. It was another warm April day and I got there in one lift in a sports car. The day seemed to bind together two apparent irreconcilables with which we have often been aware of living since, a sense of awed uncertainty about the future and a sense of thrilled joy at the loving reality of God. In the tube I found myself reflecting again on passages of Scripture that had come home to me over the previous week: 'For to me, to live is Christ' (Phil. 1:21) and 'there is nothing upon earth that I desire besides thee' (Ps. 73:25 RSV), and on the hymn that says, 'Thou, O Christ, art all I want'.

The corticotrophin did its trick and within a fortnight Ann was back to normal. A year later, just before we were married, the problem recurred, and the treatment worked again. At the beginning of 1968 we discovered Ann was pregnant and her neurologist said it was risky for her to proceed with the pregnancy; she should have an abortion. We asked to see another neurologist, who was inclined to agree, but who commented – Ann doesn't remember this bit, but I don't think I invented it – that, while it was evident from her case notes that she had the illness, he could find no trace of it in her when he examined her. He could not remember seeing someone who had had two severe attacks of the illness, as Ann evidently had, and who was now as well as she was. That was enough evidence of God being at work for us. Ann went through a fairly uneventful pregnancy and the young man who should have been flushed down the toilet is now 5ft 10, half way through university, and this weekend hosting a speaker round Greenbelt.

As far as I recall, the next decade was fairly uneventful, except for an amusing experience in 1975. Ann became ill again, when our GP happened to be on holiday. Another doctor decided to try a different form of the corticotrophin treatment, involving a more concentrated dosage. As a side effect this sent Ann off her head – manic, to use the term she prefers: she became over-active, wanting to do all sorts of things that she really hadn't got the strength to complete. It was a good experience for someone who had begun postgraduate training as a psychiatrist. As one aspect of the mania, she would wake each sunny May morning at five o'clock with messages from God in her head. These were 'obviously' psychotic delusions. The difficulty about this analysis was that she would then find the same message from God in similar words in the Scripture Union readings for the day. These came from the Psalms. The one I recall is the picture in Psalm 126 of the Lord restoring fortunes and people being like dreamers, their mouths filled with laughter and their tongues with joy. Ann had gone through a spiritually dry period, and the bout of the illness – and the mania! – brought just that experience of the Lord restoring, in a way that she couldn't have dreamt would happen.

Multiple sclerosis is an unpredictable illness. Over a long period of years it responded so well to corticotrophin that many people who didn't happen to meet Ann during one of the relapses were unaware that she had the illness. We see the caring hand of God in the fact that she was so well through the years of our boys' childhood. In 1979 she completed postgraduate training in psychiatry, gained Membership of the Royal College of Psychiatrists, and began further training in psychotherapy. In 1980, however, the pattern of the illness changed; since then the relapses have been more frequent, and while the corticotrophin has continued to be effective, it is not 100% so. At the same time, the effects of these relapses have been compounded by a more gradual decline in Ann's mobility, so that she now walks only short distances, with a stick, has difficulty driving, and is limited in the work she can do. Obviously it has been a hard experience for me to watch her lose the ability to live a full human life and to fulfil the vocation at which she was skilled.

The years in which that has been going on have been ones in which I have come to experience and appreciate more fully aspects of charismatic renewal. I have not been 'baptized in the Spirit', nor do I speak in tongues – or perform 'signs and wonders'! But I have been drawn into a greater 'openness to God', sense of God, expectancy of his working, and willingness to take risks in prayer and ministry (including ministry of healing). We have been prayed with and ministered to on a number of occasions in connection with Ann's illness, sometimes by people who work within a 'signs and wonders' framework. We have seen answers to prayer and have seen God working in connection with Ann's illness, but not by stopping its progress. The answers and the miracles are of another kind. I know that having to live with it has changed me, making me more open to other people as well as more open to God. I know that it is sometimes out of what God has given me through Ann's illness that I minister. In a way that makes living with the experience worse; it makes God more awesome. I also know that just by her presence Ann in her weakness, her vulnerability, and her courage brings something to situations, even something of Christ. And that is also difficult to live with, because I also know that she does not find in herself that suffering draws her nearer to God, at least at the moment. I know that it has all made Christian hope more important to us both: I look forward to seeing Ann dance in heaven, let alone walk.

It will become apparent from the chapters that follow that people's own experience of healing ministry contributes significantly to the way they see these issues. That is the case with the editor, too, no doubt; so that is the background he is aware of bringing to the debate. The theses and the questions that follow are written against the background of that experience. For me, any theory about healing and miracle has to be able to embrace that kind of – quite regular – human experience.

JOHN GOLDINGAY

Some starting-points

The following theses, representing my own (sometimes tentative) position on the questions about health, suffering, healing and miracle with which this book is concerned, were put forward as a basis for discussion on the part of the contributors to the volume, with a view to clarifying areas of agreement and disagreement. Each pair of authors was asked to concentrate on one section and to take up the theses, texts and questions that most seemed to require discussion.

Health, suffering and healing

1. God's creation purpose was that humanity should enjoy fullness of life in all its interrelated aspects – spiritual, social, mental and physical. Inevitably the spoiling of our relationship with God meant us losing the other aspects of full life, and ultimately losing life itself.

2. The process of ageing, however, which includes aspects of disease, seems to be built into the nature of humanity; it need not stem from our rebellion against God (it may have been God's purpose to grant us resurrection life on completion of our 'natural' created lifespan). Thus some experience of the limitations that age and degener-ation bring to faculties such as memory, eyesight and

hearing may be God's will for us. His best for us is then that we enjoy the health appropriate to our age and to his calling. This may be different from our health earlier in our lives, or from the experience of other people whom he purposes to use in different ways.

3. Similarly, not all pain and suffering need result from the entry of sin into the world, and therefore be evils to be fought against. The subduing of the world to which humanity was commissioned (Gn. 1:28) might have been expected to include an element of these, and pain would have been associated with childbirth even if no-one had sinned. Nevertheless, sin did bring about a death which would otherwise have been unnecessary, and an increase in pain and suffering.

4. God's purpose in Christ is to give us that fullness of life in all its interrelated aspects which he originally intended for us. Healing as well as forgiveness is the fruit of his work (see Mt. 8:17 with its allusion to Is. 53). He has done all that was needed to make fullness of life in all aspects available to us.

5. He restored wholeness in different dimensions to many people during his ministry; often these dimensions were interwoven (see Mk. 2:1–12: forgiveness and healing; Mk. 10:25: healing and following Jesus). He commissioned his disciples to minister this wholeness on his behalf. He also saw demonic activity behind some sickness he came across; his response was to rebuke the evil spirit and thus to heal the person (see *e.g.* Lk. 8:26–33).

6. Sometimes people's faith led to their being healed (see Mk. 5:34), and it may be that faith on the part of *someone* was always needed if a person was to be healed (see Mt. 13:58), but faith on the part of the sick themselves does not always feature (see Mk. 2:5; *cf*. Jas. 5:15).

7. Jesus's healing ministry, that of the disciples, and that exercised in Acts, demonstrate that Jesus's coming brings a New Age. This ministry is reported as part of the gospel; it is not set forth as a model for our ministry. Where Jesus does commission the church after his resurrection, healing is not mentioned (except in the later ending to Mark).

Healing in the gospels and Acts should, then, not be made the fundamental basis for our understanding of healing ministry today.

8. Although Christ achieved all that was needed to restore us to wholeness, Christians still live in this age, and enjoy only part of that fullness of life destined for them. We still live in hope, awaiting our redemption (Rom. 8:23–24).

9. Some aspects of this shortfall stem from our disobedience, our stupidity (*e.g.* over diet or exercise), and our failure to lay hold on all the potential available to us in Christ. Other aspects reflect the fact that God himself does not purpose to complete our re-creation until the End of all things.

10. In New Testament times sickness sometimes had to be accepted (see Phil. 2:26; 2 Tim. 4:20); God did not grant every prayer for healing (see 2 Cor. 12:7–10). Paul suggests what looks like recourse to ordinary medical treatment for Timothy's ailments (1 Tim. 5:23).

11. Some New Testament passages affirm the positive value of suffering, which presumably includes ill-health (see Rom. 5:3–5; Jas. 1:2–4). The Book of Job explicitly warns against assuming that believers will not experience ill-health or can expect immediate relief if ill-health should come; and the Psalms make the same assumption. Hebrews 12 suggests that believers should expect to experience God's discipline, not uninterrupted health, wealth and ease.

12. Thus in church history and in current Christian experience many have been brought to personal and spiritual maturity through coping with adversity and pressure, including ill-health, rather than through calm, ease, and the removal of every pain and hurt.

Questions

A   Is our experience of pain and sickness entirely the result of sin spoiling the world's relationship with God? Or can some pain and sickness be intended by God for our blessing?

B   If the latter, how do we tell what is the significance of a particular experience of pain or illness?

C   In what sense does healing come to us through Christ's work on the cross?

D   How much of the fruit of salvation can we expect to enjoy now, and how much belongs inevitably to the End? How does this apply to suffering and healing?

E   What is the relation between faith and healing?

F   What is the relation between the demonic and sickness, and how does this affect our approach to healing?

G   What is the significance of the story of Job in connection with our understanding of God's purpose regarding suffering and healing?

Healing and miracle

13. In English, 'miracle' has two chief meanings, neither of which exactly corresponds to any biblical expressions. It sometimes denotes an 'event inexplicable by natural laws and so ascribed to divine or supernatural action' (*Penguin English Dictionary*). Jesus's resurrection would be a clear example.

14. This is commonly the word's connotation when used today in connection with healing. Some of Jesus's healings and some events in Acts would clearly be 'miracles' in this sense.

15. Yet events that we can describe in terms of 'laws of nature' (that is, we can perceive the process whereby they came about) and ones we cannot are equally the work of God.

16. Further, it is impossible to establish that a particular event *was* a miracle, in the sense that it could never be explained in terms of ordinary processes of cause and effect (including some processes yet to be discovered).

17. We also have to allow that many illnesses (*e.g.* most cancers) are known in a small percentage of cases to recede or even to disappear 'naturally'.

18. For various reasons, then, it is best to avoid using the term 'miracle' with regard to healings today.

19. In everyday speech 'miracle' can also denote something which is remarkable and extraordinary, but is not

assumed to require explanation in terms of supernatural activity. Many biblical 'signs and wonders' might be remarkable and extraordinary events which were, however, no more (and no less) 'supernatural' than other events. Exodus gives the crossing of the Red Sea a 'natural' explanation (it involved a strong east wind). Such events might still appropriately be described as 'miraculous' because they happened at particularly significant moments not only for those who received them, but for the purpose of God himself as he went about fulfilling his purpose in the world. They are signs and wonders, but are also capable of scientific description and explanation.

20. Some healing 'miracles' might also be of this kind. For instance, the paralysis of the man in Mark 2 may have resulted from his inner sense of guilt, so that the resolution of the latter (his 'inner healing') 'naturally' made it possible for him to walk again. This healing is still, of course, the marvellous work of *God*.

21. It is also God who brings healing through the regular healing processes at work in the body and who enables people to understand these processes and harness them by means of medicine, surgery, *etc*. Such healings are not 'miracles', but they are still the work of God (and may seem marvellous indeed when we come to understand them).

22. Thus the appropriate reaction to illness is *both* prayer *and* recourse to physical medicine: the latter can be an act of unfaith (2 Ch. 16:12), but it can belong in the context of faith in God (2 Ki. 20:1–7). There is no tension or competition between God's two ways of bringing healing; he may use either.

23. As in Mark 2, we should not be surprised if many healings can be explained in psychosomatic terms. This does not make them any less 'signs and wonders'.

24. The gospels and Acts show that being confronted by 'signs and wonders' does not compel people to faith in Christ. Other explanations can always be thought of. To recognize an experience of healing as an expression of God's power and love and a sign of his presence is a response of faith.

Questions

H   How do you see the relation between healing by the resources of physical medicine, and healing through prayer and seeking God 'direct'?

I   How do you see the relation between 'natural' and 'supernatural' in people's gifts of healing or special insight?

J   When we are ill, how do we decide whether to seek the resources of physical medicine or those of prayer and seeking God's 'direct' healing?

K   Both Scripture and subsequent history indicate that extraordinary healings can be brought about in the name of other gods or of demonic powers. Does this diminish the significance of signs and wonders? If not, why not?

L   In what sense does Jesus encourage his disciples to expect to do greater things than he did (Jn. 14:12)?

Healing in church life

25. In New Testament times, in the course of ordinary church life Christians were expected to offer a ministry of physical and mental healing as well as concerning themselves with people's relationships with God. This might involve people with special gifts (1 Cor. 12), but it was also part of regular pastoral ministry (Jas. 5:13–16). There is no reference to the rebuking of evil spirits in the course of ordinary church life in New Testament times.

26. The New Testament offers no examples of people with gifts of healing going round carrying out healing missions. Elders and people with gifts of healing fulfilled this ministry within congregations; apostles and evangelists combined healing with preaching the gospel. This may be significant for our understanding of both the role of the evangelist and that of the healer.

27. It is clear from a passage such as James 5:13–16 that medically unexpected healings were part of the life of the church in New Testament times, and presumably this should also be so today.

28. It is also clear from 1 Corinthians 12 that some early Christian churches included people who had 'gifts

of healing', and presumably this, too, should be the case today.

29. Such gifts might be of an explicitly supernatural kind (transcending what the person could otherwise do); they might be personal qualities and abilities given over to God for his service but inherently part of the person exercising them (so that the person would be able to do something like this even if he or she was not a Christian).

Questions

M   In what sense and on what basis can we take the signs and wonders performed by Jesus, his disciples, and the church in Acts as a guide to the healing ministry we should expect to see exercised in the church today?

N   What is the place of the ministry of healing in the life of the church? Does the ministry of healing belong in the context of regular public worship, or of special services, or in the home, or of healing missions, or of healing centres, or what?

O   In what way should we expect 'signs and wonders' to witness to God's presence and power? How does such ministry relate to evangelism?

P   Is it our business to attempt to discern when God might wish to do some 'sign' by healing someone? If so, how do we do so?

Q   Is it our business to attempt to distinguish between divine healing in answer to prayer, and 'spontaneous remission'? If so, how do we do so?

R   What do you understand by the term 'inner healing', and how do you see the role of this ministry in the church today? How does the ministry of inner healing relate to that of physical healing?

S   What is the place for the rebuking of evil spirits in connection with healing ministry?

T   James 5:13–16 seems to encourage us to assume that healing will always follow upon anointing, believing prayer, and confession. When it does not, are we to infer that there must have been an absence of faith on the part of the elders, or that 'the prayer of faith' is a special God-given assurance that God will heal *in this case*, or that the passage encourages us to expect that the kind of person it is talking about will always be 'saved' whether or not he or she is 'healed'? Or what?

JOHN GOLDINGAY

Part 1
Health, suffering and healing

Peter May and Tony Dale

Focusing on the eternal

Seeing God at work in the physical

Focusing on the eternal

Peter May

What is health? · Shalom · Shalom characterized the experience of life before the fall and will be the experience of the redeemed in heaven. We experience it now in part through the gift of new life of Christ · People in God's image. Christ restores this image. In the present world the restoration is spiritual not physical, as death is inevitable · The concept of spiritual health. This has effects on society and the environment. It is the Christian's changed life-style which helps the environment and the body · Healing can only be partial · The atonement · Healing in the New Testament · Christ's statement 'greater things . . .' · Our response to suffering · Miraculous signs and wonders are not normative for the Christian

What is health?

The word itself derives from the Anglo-Saxon word *hal* meaning 'whole'. Definitions of health are often given in negative terms such as 'the state of being *free from* disease mentally and physically'. Clearly it is not adequate to define health just in physical terms, nor should it be defined just in terms of the absence of other things. The World Health Organization has a definition which is both broad and positive, 'a state of complete physical, mental and social well-being and not merely an absence of disease'. The Christian however will want to qualify the definition further. True health in God's world must include spiritual well-being; *complete* well-being however is to anticipate heaven.

The Bible word that most closely expresses these ideas

is 'shalom'. Meaning 'completeness, soundness, well-being', it describes a positive experience of peace and fulfilment. Jerusalem itself derives its name from shalom, probably meaning 'a city of peace'. The Psalmist (Ps. 122) implies that security, prosperity and justice all contribute to shalom. Isaiah speaks of shalom when he prophesies, ' "I live . . . with him who is contrite and lowly in spirit . . . I will heal him; I will guide him and restore comfort to him . . . Peace (shalom), peace, to those far and near." . . . But the wicked are like the tossing sea, which cannot rest . . . "There is no peace (shalom)," says my God, "for the wicked" ' (Is. 57:15, 18–21). The Prince of Peace (Is. 9:6) wept over Jeru-shalom: 'If you, even you, had only known on this day what would bring you peace – but now it is hidden from your eyes . . . You did not recognise the time of God's coming to you' (Lk. 19:42, 44).

I take it that this all-round shalom characterized the experience of life before the fall and will be the experience of the redeemed in heaven. That we experience it now in part is the wonder of the new life Isaiah predicted and which Jesus offers us – a life which does not consist of the abundance of our possessions but of our life in friendship with our creator and sustainer. The gift of the Holy Spirit brings us a real experience of that peace which the world cannot give, and makes our relationship with God a personal, spiritual reality.

Health then in an absolute sense was something Adam and Eve experienced before their disobedience, and is something the redeemed will experience in the new creation. In the interim, we can only experience relative health which fluctuates by degree. It is quite inappropriate to speak of healing as though it were a final event, or think of health as a state which is available to us fully now.

That health is multi-faceted is seen more clearly if we consider healing in terms of restoring the 'image of God' in us. The church has long debated the full significance of this phrase. Generally it is agreed that it carries the implication that man is a moral creature, but frequently it is seen to embrace much more than our moral faculties.

The phrase first occurs in Genesis 1:26. At the climax of creation, God having made the animals to his own satisfaction goes on to create a different being who is made actually like *himself*. The two criteria for assessing what is involved in the image would appear then to be those aspects of man which mark him out from the animals and which liken him to his creator.

The likeness of God, the unlikeness of animals

Clearly the image embraces man's ability to choose right from wrong. Many want to go further than this and identify man's capacity for knowledge, intelligence, rationality, abstract thought, and ability, as it were, to step outside of himself and reflect upon his origins, purpose and destiny.

Others would emphasize man's capacity for deep personal relationships, including love and speech. Man's spiritual nature expressed in his religiosity, his capacity for awe and worship and his yearning for immortality all fit the criteria. So also would his creativity, art and ability to have dominion over other living creatures and alter his environment.

In all these areas, mankind is in a different league and usually in a different ball game from other animals. That other animals have some intelligence and other qualities is not denied. It is sufficient to observe that the differences are enormous.

Some Christian writers have gone further still and take the image of God to refer to the whole of man, body and soul (see the article 'man' in the *Illustrated Bible Dictionary*). But this I see as an error as it fits neither of the two criteria at issue. Our bodies are fundamentally unlike God who is not flesh but spirit, while at every aspect our bodies resemble animals to an extraordinary degree. Our anatomy, physiology and biochemistry only differ in small ways from our closest 'relatives' in the animal kingdom. Recent genetic discoveries have highlighted this, showing that our genes are almost identical to those of the chimpanzee! And yet man is so wonderfully different in a way that is currently inexplicable in genetic terms.

The Bible's assumption is that this image of God in us became seriously flawed when man rebelled against God. It was not however destroyed. The Christian understanding of redemption includes the restoration of this image to its former glory. Like a decaying antique, the image is rescued from the junk shop and restored to its original beauty. This process continues throughout our lives as we open ourselves up to the work of the Holy Spirit. Christ, we are told, is the unspoiled image of God (Col. 1:15, 19). He is our model and our goal. The Spirit works at restoring us to Christ-like character, and that process continues *throughout* our lives to the extent that we allow him. 'What we will be has not yet been made known. But we know that when he appears, we shall be like him, for we shall see him as he is. Everyone who has this hope in him purifies himself, just as he is pure' (1 Jn. 3:2–3).

This consideration of the image of God has set an agenda for the restoration of shalom in man which excludes man's physical body! 'Though outwardly we are wasting away, yet inwardly we are being renewed day by day,' wrote the apostle Paul. 'So we fix our eyes not on what is seen, but on what is unseen. For what is seen is temporary, but what is unseen is eternal' (2 Cor. 4:16, 18). Paul urges us to distinguish between things that differ: the outward and the inward, the visible and the invisible, the temporary and the eternal. If we get confused at this point in our quest for health, we shall never find our way out of the wood. Before we consider physical healing, let us consider briefly 'the inner man'.

Spiritual health

When Adam turned his back on God, shalom was lost. Alienation, guilt, frustration and fear flooded into his soul as he discovered evil for the first time. Whether or not Adam was destined to die in the sense of exchanging his corruptible body for an incorruptible one, now he was to face spiritual as well as physical death, the penalty his sin deserved. The judgment of God was upon him and there was nothing he could do to right the wrongs and undo the evil he had committed.

In the mercy of God, man's redemption begins with the removal of that judgment, which Christ took upon himself on the cross. The undeserved offer of forgiveness is held out to all the sons of Adam who humble themselves before God and turn from their wicked ways. Repentance and faith are the beginnings of the road back to glory. The Christian life is an outworking of all that this redemption means. The hope of heaven transforms everything, while we live out our years getting to know the creator who was once a stranger to us. To know him is to love him, to love him is to serve him and to spend our lives in pleasing him. As with all other relationships we experience, we get to know him gradually and take time to learn his ways. The relationship deepens with the years – a growth in trust, obedience, and spiritual vitality.

Social health

Our relationship with our fellows may well be in dire straits by the time we are found by Christ. However optimistic we may be about our growth in holiness, we cannot fool ourselves that restoring these human relationships is other than a long slog! Hermits and other escapists have tried to fool themselves by cutting themselves off from other people. But wholeness is not lop-sided. The inner man is renewed as he faces the difficulties and dilemmas of all his relationships and is inspired by Christ to pursue mercy, justice and compassion.

The ravages of sin may be all too evident in awkward and abrasive personalities to their dying day. No one individual can compare his progress with another. The true comparison is with his former self. Christ-like fruits may be slow to develop but are nonetheless evident. At best our social healing may be substantial, but it is never complete this side of heaven as every married person knows. Sinless perfection has at times been claimed by individuals. It is rarely assigned to them by others who know them well and have a more objective viewpoint!

Psychological health

That conversion may bring about a dramatic improvement in the integration of a personality is a common experience. That sense of peace and joy which comes from knowing that your sins have been blotted out is often so striking that family, friends and colleagues cannot ignore it. Different attitudes and responses to daily living begin from the moment of 'new birth'. A new sense of one's value before God, and the discovery of ultimate meaning and purpose, is the stuff of conversion. Yet however dramatic these changes, these new understandings and feelings have to be worked out in a complex and fallen world. Our new sensitivity of conscience may lead us to new struggles with guilt feelings. A new concern for others may bring a new sense of failing them. The renewing of our minds is a daily challenge, and hopefully a progressive experience. However, the deep traumas of the past and the difficulties of our inherited constitutions may disturb us all our days.

Physical health

While therefore we should expect renewal of the inner man, St Paul warns us that we should have no such optimism about our physical frames. 'Outwardly we are wasting away.' These physical bodies are destined to be replaced by glorious resurrection bodies which will be as different from our present forms as seeds are from the flowers which they become (1 Cor. 15:35ff.).

Physical health peaks early in life. By the time we are in our twenties our brain cells begin to die off! Aging changes in the skin appear all too soon. Degenerative 'wear and tear' changes in the joints begin in middle life, and many women enter the menopause even in their thirties. Arteries begin to harden, hairs turn grey and fall out, lung function declines and so forth.

What does it mean in purely physical terms to be healthy? Some have a strong frame and are highly intelligent. Others are weak and stupid. To speak of physical health is to discuss a relative concept. I can be healthier than most but no candidate for the decathlon. I might have healthy limbs but a congenital heart defect. I can be intelligent enough to hold down a good job but not qualify for Mensa. Similarly I can be short, weak and have a low IQ yet still be happily married and a model parent. I might be unemployable but still able to serve God in the community. Whatever my physical attributes at the age of forty, it is unlikely that any of them will have improved if I survive the next ten years.

The idea that the Christian should experience wholeness/health/salvation in any physical sense comparable to the spiritual has no place in reality and serves only to undermine his assurance of sins forgiven. Physical decay and death are inescapable parts of our current humanity. We have no grounds to expect exemption from failing eye-sight, memory, hearing, cardiac function or muscle strength. That God may extend his mercies to alleviate or cure certain illnesses in answer to our prayers is a matter for his compassion and gracious providence. That he expects our bodies to opt out of a decaying world is clearly not his general will for us.

Environmental health

To man alone among the animals has been granted 'dominion', the ability to 'lord it over' and alter our environment. Our stewardship of the created order should be transformed once we acknowledge the world's creator and begin to understand his purposes and concerns.

However, we shall not see such a transformation in the created order itself. Rather than experiencing 'growth in well-being', the world around us is 'subject to frustration' and in 'bondage to decay'. Not that God has abandoned it. Rather it is subjected thus 'in hope' of eventual liberation and re-creation (Rom. 8:18ff.).

Why should it be that there is a work of renewal inwardly while outwardly the whole of creation including our bodies is experiencing decay?

Firstly, it is a mistake to think that our renewal is greater than it is. We are not presented with the possibility of a steady progression in holiness so that in the new creation there will be only minor amendments before we are finally perfected. This would suggest that our bodies have somehow been overlooked and will be off to a late start in the process of re-creation.

Paul had a pessimistic view of his current spiritual wretchedness and drew a marked contrast between our current imperfection and the perfection that is to come. Now we see but a poor reflection; then we shall see face to face.

Secondly, the general picture is that the current order is under judgment and destined to pass away. However, through the death of Jesus it is under judgment but with a promise. The promise is for a full salvation involving a new heaven and earth, involving a holy people clothed in resurrection bodies. But all that is part of the 'not yet'.

Great expectations?

What then can we expect now? The world is under judgment and we are told to wait patiently for the liberation that is promised.

'For the creation was subjected to frustration, not by its own choice, but by the will of the one who subjected it, in hope that the creation itself will be liberated from its bondage to decay and brought into the glorious freedom of the children of God' (Rom. 8:20–21). However, God in his mercy has given us a down-payment, a pledge of what lies ahead of us: 'He . . . set his seal of ownership on us, and put his Spirit in our hearts as a deposit, guaranteeing what is to come' (2 Cor. 1:22).

The Holy Spirit then does not bring us full salvation now, but merely a foretaste of what is to come. Renewal is real but it is not complete by any means. Decay is the order of the day, but the Spirit in our hearts is a pledge of the renewal that lies ahead. So Paul wrote in Romans 8: 'We . . . who have the firstfruits of the Spirit, groan inwardly as we wait eagerly for our adoption as sons, the redemption of our bodies. For in this hope we were saved. But hope that is seen is no hope at all. Who hopes for what he already has? But if we hope for what we do not yet have, we wait for it patiently' (vv. 23–25). Paul makes it quite clear that the redemption of our bodies is something we must wait for patiently.

In 1 Corinthians 15 the body is likened to a seed which must die. The flowering of the new resurrection body awaits us after death. In the current order we shall experience outward decay (2 Cor. 4:16). All our bodily functions will deteriorate by degree. Currently the writer is developing grey hairs, is going bald and has recently had to resort to using reading glasses. The number of my brain cells is declining and my arterial walls are presumably thickening, though I hope that neither of these is currently obvious! I can have no other expectation than a gradual deterioration of my physical health in the years ahead.

Does the Christian then have any better expectation of health than the non-Christian? Certainly we should escape some illnesses through the nature of our life-style. We are told to treat our bodies with the respect that God's temple deserves. Consequently most of us do not smoke cigarettes nor consume alcohol excessively. Our sexual morality reduces the risk of AIDS to a minimum along with other sexually related diseases such as cervical cancer. We should not be subject to gluttony and are motivated to battle with obesity! The prevailing wisdom should encourage us to pursue a high-fibre diet with all its attendant benefits. We should also be alerted to the benefits of regular exercise.

However, I have no grounds for expecting to be bypassed by a major 'flu epidemic or other similar infectious outbreaks. Keeping my body healthy may increase my resistance and ability to throw off such illnesses. Neither am I immune to life's stresses even if my spiritual life gives me resources in handling them. Our fallen natures persist to the grave and many Christians become depressed by their sins. Job however became depressed not by his sins but by his circumstances and there is nothing in the Bible to suggest that God's people will be preserved from sadness and tragedy. Sudden infant deaths and early onset of diabetes can be expected to occur equally in the Christian and non-Christian communities. The devastating Reye's Syndrome appears to be related to aspirin ingestion rather than moral factors and as none of us can choose the families that we are born into neither can we escape our share of inherited disease. We seem to be equally at risk from most types of cancer and once these diseases have got a hold of us our cure rate appears to be no different from anyone else's.

What then can we say about 'health'? Surely we should be under no illusions about it. It belongs ultimately to another world. Now we experience it by measure only. Inwardly, by the renewing of our minds and the work of the Spirit we can experience renewal, growth and health in our *relationships* with God, ourselves, our fellows and our environment. Yet outwardly, our bodies and our environment are part of a decaying system. But worse than that, the outer world constantly interacts with the inner self. Our labours bring tiredness, bereavement brings depression, relationships bring tension, old age brings dementia and the decaying of our renewed minds. Lies deceive us, wickedness tempts us, evil men may persecute us and even mutilate us.

It is in this turbulent groaning of life that God gives us his peace which the world cannot give. It is in a sinful world that we are called to grow in holiness, in an alienating world that we are to restore relationships, in an often chaotic environment that we are called to be stewards and have dominion. Our well-being, our health, our experience of shalom, real as it is, occurs only in part – a downpayment and promise of the 'health' that is to come.

Healing

If that is the best we can say about health then what can we say about healing? Just this – that at best in any area of our being it is only partial. Amputated limbs stop bleeding but don't regrow. Mental breakdowns settle but emotional scars remain. The sins of our parents take their toll on our upbringing and we can never relive those formative years. Congenital diseases leave us incapacitated for life and our genetic constitution is not going to be reformed this side of heaven. (A well-known evangelist claimed to a large audience to have healed a boy with Down's Syndrome. He withdrew his claim on subsequent correspondence.) We are promised no immunity from familial diseases, whether trivial like baldness or catastrophic like Huntingdon's Chorea. Our personalities and constitutions are shaped genetically and by our upbringing. The Bible offers us no personality transplants in the here and now. We will not undergo genetic reconstruction nor be able to eliminate the effects of a disturbed childhood.

None of this is to belittle God's gracious work in us. He takes such raw material and shapes it. He does not however change it in this life into different material. It is not that he cannot change a Down's Syndrome child or restore the intellect of a demented man, but it is evident that such transformation is not part of his current purposes for us.

Healing in the New Testament

The gospels however clearly describe the most extraordinary wonders at the hands of Jesus. The king of creation stilled the storm and healed the paralytic. He walked on water and gave sight to a man born blind. He turned water into wine and restored a withered hand. He fed 5,000 and raised the dead. The apostle John called such things 'signs' and recorded them that we 'may believe that Jesus is the Christ, the Son of God' (Jn. 20:31).

The apostles also performed great signs. 'The things that mark an apostle,' said Paul, '– signs, wonders, and miracles – were done among you with great perseverance' (2 Cor. 12:12). None of these wonders was greater than those of Christ. The apostles also performed far fewer, it seems. Once we get beyond Acts and into the epistles there is hardly a mention about physical health and healing. In particular, the silence in Ephesians and the Pastoral Epistles (which concern the church and its ministry) is *deafening.* An ambiguous reference in only one of the lists of gifts, to the 'gifts of healings' (double plural), and the passage in James 5 which is more about intercessory prayer than signs and wonders, have to be weighed against the recorded instances of illness. Trophimus would not have been left at Miletus (2 Tim. 4:20), nor Paul have preached in Galatia (Gal. 4:13) if they had not been struck down with illnesses. Epaphroditus was so sick he nearly died (Phil. 2:27ff.) and Timothy had no supernatural answer to his gastric complaints (1 Tim. 5:23).

This last reference is especially interesting. We are told that Timothy, a key Christian leader, suffered frequent illnesses. Paul recommends that he uses a little wine (perhaps to stimulate his appetite, or was the water contaminated?). But he does not advocate the 'laying on of hands' although he has used this phrase in the previous sentence (v. 22).

It seems clear that Paul's thorn in the flesh was a physical illness, whether epilepsy, malaria, bad eyesight or something else. (Certainly his eyesight appears to have been bad – see Gal. 4:15; 6:11; Acts 23:3–5). Whatever he meant by his thorn, he not only learnt to live with it, but he found in his weakness the key to his spiritual strength. 'Three times I pleaded with the Lord to take it away from me. But he said to me, "My grace is sufficient for you, for my power is made perfect in weakness." ' Neither did Paul tolerate his sufferings begrudgingly. 'Therefore I will boast all the more gladly about my weaknesses, so that Christ's power may rest on me. That is why, for Christ's sake, I delight in weaknesses, in insults, in hardships, in persecutions, in difficulties. For when I am weak, then I am strong' (2 Cor. 12:8–10).

Healing and the atonement

It is often suggested that Christ's death on the cross was to bring us physical health quite as much as forgiveness. Matthew 8:17 is called upon to support this idea. Quoting the prophet Isaiah (53:4) the text reads, 'He took up our infirmities and carried our diseases.' The passage is directly linked in people's minds with the atonement, for Isaiah goes on to speak of the suffering servant being crushed for our iniquities (Is. 53:5). However Matthew says that the verse he has quoted has already been fulfilled, not in Christ's death but in his life as he healed all the sick people who were brought to him. The passage points to the significance of Christ's healing miracles as signs that he is the promised Messiah.

The memorial meal as instituted by Christ and passed on by Paul bears no reference to healing in the atonement. 'This is my blood of the covenant, which is poured out for many for the forgiveness of sins' (Mt. 26:28; *cf.* 1 Cor. 11:23ff.). Neither does Paul mention healing when he lists those things which were of 'first importance' (1 Cor. 15:3): 'Christ died for our sins according to the Scriptures', he wrote.

It is true that 1 Peter 2:24 quotes Isaiah 53:5 in a statement about the atonement: 'He himself bore our sins in his body on the tree, so that we might die to sins and live for righteousness; by his wounds you have been healed.' The context is plainly about the moral and spiritual implications of Christ's death, achieving our forgiveness that we might 'live for righteousness', and it would be clutching at straws to read physical health into this.

The great commission

The twelve apostles were given a particular charge which included healing (Mt. 10:8) but in a definitely limited context. They were told specifically not to go among the Gentiles nor to visit any Samaritan town. Later the Lord commissioned seventy-two to go ahead of him as an advance party. They were specifically told to go to every town and place where Jesus was about to go (Lk. 10:1). Luke records the end of both tours where the disciples reported back to their master (Lk. 9:10; 10:17). We do not read in the gospels of the disciples performing miracles apart from such special commissionings. Their ministry was part of the gospel announcement of the coming of the King and the dawning of the new age. It was not set forth as a pattern for our ministry, and when Jesus commissioned the church after the resurrection, healing was not mentioned. Neither should this surprise us, for after these healing tours both Matthew and Luke record Christ's dreadful rebuke: 'A wicked and adulterous generation asks for a miraculous sign! But none will be given it except the sign of the prophet Jonah', a reference to his resurrection (Mt. 12:39–40; Lk. 11:29).

The only passage which appears to contradict this is Mark 16:17–18. This version of the great commission certainly does speak of 'accompanying signs' and says that believers will 'place their hands on sick people and they will get well'. However, the most reliable early manuscripts of Mark's Gospel stop at 16:8. It is clear that the subsequent verses were not part of the original account, as modern versions of the Bible make clear. It would be a dubious foundation for a major thesis and has no parallel in the commission of Matthew 28:18–20 or for that matter Luke 24:47–48, John 20:21–23 or Acts 1:8.

'As the Father has sent me . . .'

Some have appealed to John 20:21 where Christ told the disciples that he was sending them out as the Father had sent himself. They argue that as Christ performed miracles, so should his followers. However, it would seem arbitrary from that reading to select only the healing signs. Should his disciples also walk on water and still storms, occasionally be transfigured and be able to predict future events? Surely no sane person would argue that any Christian would be entirely like the incarnate Christ! What then is the point of similarity? As he represented the Father in the world, so they are to represent their Lord (Lightfoot). Doing so there are numerous points of similarity between Christ's mission and theirs. But to suggest their mission is identical is absurd. They are not called upon to die for the sins of the world, nor appear as lords of the created order. They are not calling men to themselves nor should they presume to have the mighty power of God at their fingertips. No matter how important their mission, they remain mortal, fallen humankind.

Greater things?

Surely Jesus said that his disciples would do 'greater things' than he did (Jn. 14:12)? It seems to me to be extraordinarily inept that anyone can think that the greater things refer to his miracles, even though they are mentioned in the previous verse. These things were signs precisely because of their uniqueness. But what greater signs could possibly be performed? Has anyone walked on air, stilled a hurricane, turned water into champagne, fed 20,000 from three loaves and one fish? Of course not! Neither have any healing miracles ever occurred which were *greater* than the healings of Christ. Indeed my own researches over many years have never revealed anything remotely comparable. That is not of course to say that they cannot or don't happen. It is to say that miracles similar to the ones performed by Christ in terms of their immediacy, completeness and astonishing nature must anyway be very rare indeed.

Despite the plethora of claims currently being made, most Christian healers today will admit how rare such things are in their own experience. No. The greater things do not relate to the miracles of verse 11, but the Father's *work* referred to in verse 10. 'Anyone who has faith in me will do what I have been doing. He will do even greater things than these, because I am going to the Father.' It has I believe to do with foot-washing (Jn. 13:14), loving one another (Jn. 13:34) and heroic self-sacrifice (Jn. 13:38). It has to do with the great work that Jesus came into the world to do, to establish the kingly rule of God among men – gospel work, reconciling work. All these things can be done in an altogether greater way after Christ's atoning death and the gift of his Holy Spirit to mobilize a mighty army to take his love to the ends of the earth.

Gospel priorities

In the first chapter of Mark's gospel, Jesus is reported to have healed a demon-possessed man. Without modern means of communication, the news spread like wildfire and soon the whole town was at his door (Mk. 1:28, 33). He healed many of them, but escaped early next morning to a solitary place. Simon went after him and (surprise, surprise) told him, 'Everyone is looking for you!' Jesus replied, 'Let us go somewhere else so that I can preach there also. That is why I have come' (Mk. 1:37–38).

The next reported healing of a physical illness – leprosy, which was healed immediately and completely – was followed by a strong warning: 'See that you don't tell this to anyone.' But instead the man told everyone. 'As a result, Jesus could no longer enter a town openly but stayed outside in lonely places' (Mk. 1:40–45).

If someone in Britain could heal AIDS instantaneously and completely – or even indisputably heal just *one case* – the crush would be enormous. The congestion at Heathrow from multitudes flying in from Africa and the USA would be headline news. But they cannot. Obviously the Lord could work such miracles, but he does not appear to be willing to do so (*cf.* Mk. 1:40). Why is it that so many of the reported healings seem to be at a purely trivial and subjective level, such as backache, while cleft palates or proven secondary cancers such as David Watson's remain uncured? News of such healings would be every-where, whereas I have not been able to find one medically convincing case. The Lord does not seem to be willing, and I presume that his reluctance now is for the same reason as his reluctance then. It would be a distraction and obstacle to the work of evangelism. It is the gospel of eternal salvation that our world needs, not temporary respite for our ailing bodies. There is no greater work than this.

Our response to suffering

In a general sense it is easy to see that the vast amount of the world's suffering is directly or indirectly due to mankind. Many illnesses are directly the result of wicked-ness such as violence, gluttony, sexual licence or guilt. A given illness may be the direct result of doing something we know to be wrong. It may be due to the sins of our parents or spouse, or be in a more general sense the result of fallen humanity. 'Son, your sins are forgiven,' said Jesus to the paralysed man. 'Get up, take your mat and go home' (Mk. 2:5, 11). Similarly Paul warned, 'That is why many among you are weak and sick, and a number of you have fallen asleep' (1 Cor. 11:30). Hence many illnesses should cause us to examine ourselves and see if our behaviour or attitudes have resulted in the dis-ease.

It is the plain teaching of Christ, however, and indeed the story of Job, that our sufferings are by no means always related to our sins (Lk. 13:2–5). Job was singled out for special treatment from Satan precisely because he was blameless and upright before God (Jb. 1:8). Job's comforters endlessly taunted him about his sins which they thought had precipitated God's wrath, but Job knew nothing in his life to account for it. Yet his suffering brought him to the depths of despair (Jb. 17:13–15).

Some illnesses are clearly not our fault but are allowed by God for a good purpose. That is how Paul understood his 'thorn'. His illness in Galatia had similarly positive repercussions. The apostle tells us that 'in all things God works for the good of those who love him, who have been called according to his purpose' (Rom. 8:28).

The story of Joseph is a marvellous example of an evil committed by his brothers causing enormous suffering to Joseph and his father Jacob, which God used in his sovereign purposes for the good of the entire family and their descendants (Gn. 50:20). So it is right that Christians should first of all search their hearts to see if some disobedience has caused their illness, and they should reflect upon God's wider purpose to see what good can come of it. But herein lies a problem.

It was presumably many years before Joseph could see the good purposes of God at work, while Job was never to see any 'cash value' for his suffering. The desire to find some good in wretched circumstances *can* lead Christians to try to justify God. What amount of good can they achieve to balance the books? Perhaps a bereavement might open a ministry for them among those who mourn, but how many people do they need to counsel to justify the loss God has allowed to happen? That our suffering among other circumstances is used by God for our guidance is one thing. The need to create some good out of it can lead to a frenzied quest to justify the tragedy. Job's suffering remained a mystery to him. The fact that his agonizing has been a challenge and comfort to God's people ever since is presumably something he could never have known. Frequently there will be no evident 'cash value' for our pains. Having searched our hearts for faults that need repentance, and considered for our comfort and encouragement what good may flow from our adversity (and it's an ill wind that blows no one any good!), the Christian response should rather be: How can I get back on my feet and continue to follow Christ as I was doing beforehand? Others may see in us a greater humility and sympathy; history may reveal some grand design; yet for the most part the challenge before us is to put our faith in the good purposes of God whether we understand those purposes or not. We are after all called to live by faith and not by sight.

The rain we are told falls on the just and the unjust. Influenza appears to spread with a similar lack of regard for moral distinction. Our pains and discomforts are all part of our lot as members of a fallen humanity. That is not to say that God is not merciful to his people and doesn't frequently answer specific prayers to alleviate the distress of the saints. But he does not give us a free passport to a tranquil life. Not only do we have to face our own trials and tragedies, but in taking up our cross we are asked to share the tragedies of others. Often the very reason we can weep with those who weep is that we have suffered similar pains ourselves.

Conclusion

Neither Scripture nor medical experience encourages belief that miraculous signs and wonders should be expected as a normative phenomenon in the church of any age. The current emphasis on healing encourages a neuroticism that focuses attention on the outward, the visible and the temporary to the neglect of the inward, the invisible and the eternal. It distracts us from the positive value of suffering. Paul tells us we should be able to rejoice in our sufferings 'because we know that suffering produces perseverance; perseverance, character; and character, hope. And hope does not disappoint us, because God has poured out his love into our hearts by the Holy Spirit whom he has given to us' (Rom. 5:3–5). Furthermore, concern for signs and wonders focuses on the immediate and spectacular to the neglect of care for the chronically sick. It causes false expectations about health and the nature of salvation, and undermines the assurance of those who remain unhealed. The importance of these things for the spiritual health of the church is very great indeed.

Response to Peter May

The kingdom now
and not yet

Tony Dale

What is this kingdom?

A tension seems to me to underline the profound difference of expectation between Dr Peter May's chapter and my own which follows. The tension is between differing understandings of the kingdom of God and the degree to which we live in and experience this kingdom now. That God quite frequently does heal is nowadays really beyond speculation. Unless we feel that those who are reporting extraordinary accounts of the miraculous in various Third World countries, let alone folk like myself who have seen the Lord do a considerable amount of healing in this country, are lying, then we have little reason to doubt what God can do. If one wants documentation of God's healing power from well attested sources, one can probably do little better than to read *Healing Miracles* by Rex Gardiner (FRCOG). However, the question is not what God *can* do, but what God *will* do. Where do we draw the line between understanding what is ordinarily available to the Christian and what is only available as an extraordinary manifestation of grace?

I believe the issue is clearly set out by our Lord in what we call 'The Lord's Prayer': 'Thy Kingdom come, Thy will be done, on earth as it is in heaven.' We know that in heaven there is neither sickness nor dying, neither sorrow nor pain (see, for example, Rev. 21:4). A part of our task, as outposts of the kingdom of God on earth, is to be actively praying that the reality of that kingdom rule which is now perfectly manifest in heaven enters our earthly situations. It is obviously going to be a matter of both battle and perseverance for an open manifestation of this kingdom to come, whether it is in terms of 'righteousness, peace and joy in the Holy Spirit' (Rom. 14:17), or in the casting out of demons (Lk. 11:20). Both are equally manifestations of the presence of the kingdom. Both are areas where we need to be involved aggressively in taking hold of ground certainly ours because of the finished work of Christ, but which will only be captured in this life as we pursue the Lord.

The Christian walk is not passive. Although Jesus is our righteousness, we are still commanded to 'Pursue righteousness'. Although he is our peace, we are still told to 'pursue peace with all men'. Equally it is plain that 'he is our life'. This does not take away our necessity to reach out to him for this life. The degree to which we manifest the kingdom of God is going to depend on the extent to which we allow God's Word to take root in our heart. God's Word is equally valid to all people at all times. However it only produces fruit in our individual lives when it is mixed with faith. The writer to the Hebrews remarks (4:1–2), 'Therefore, since the promise of entering his rest still stands, let us be careful that none of you be found to have fallen short of it. For we also have had the gospel preached to us, just as they did; but the message they heard was of no value to them, because those who heard it did not combine it with faith. Now we who have believed enter that rest.'

Jesus taught us clearly that the kingdom of God suffers violence and that the violent take it by force (Mt. 11:12). We obviously play an integral part in this earthly manifestation of God's rule. This is typical of the whole realm of prayer warfare and what the Lord has taught us of prayer. Surely, it is not God who is changing as we pray, but we ourselves. Even as we pray, 'Thy Kingdom come, Thy will be done', we are effectively saying, 'Lord, change me so that I can help extend the reality and answer of that prayer'.

Perhaps I can illustrate this with a situation out of my own family's experience. A number of years ago when Felicity, my wife, and I were medical students, we had the opportunity of doing an elective period in the United States. While we were there Felicity experienced a bacterial infection that was extremely painful. It was at a period in our Christian walk when we were seeking to learn much more from the Lord about healing. So rather than just take antibiotics (which would almost certainly have helped with the situation!) we felt that we should pray. In seeking the Lord he made it very plain that this infection was at a spiritual level, a direct result of something being wrong in our lives. As we asked his forgiveness and turned away from this the infection immediately cleared. However the story did not end there. A few weeks later the infection recurred. We went back to the Lord to ask him why. He made it plain that this time it was not due to any sin but so that he could manifest his glory. The Lord told Felicity that at a specific time on a specific day the pain would go and she would be healed. To that very hour, what the Lord had promised happened.

At both times we had to seek God and then pray his will into being. Is this not an expression of his command to us to pray 'Thy Kingdom come, Thy will be done, on earth as it is in heaven'?

Creation still groans

There is no doubt that Scripture makes it plain that there are limitations placed upon us. Although the sting of death has been taken away the factor of death has not been removed. Our temporal bodies have not yet put on immortality. Creation itself, as is beautifully described by Paul in Romans 8, is still subject to both futility and decay. Our bodies are not excluded.

It is interesting to note what Romans 8 says: 'The creation itself will be liberated from its bondage to decay and brought into the glorious freedom of the children of God' (v. 21). This verse seems to imply that the children of God are already enjoying a glorious liberty. The context is that of creation, *i.e.* the physical realm. One way, although certainly not the only way, of understanding this statement is that God's children are already enjoying a liberty in the physical realm which will only subsequently be shared by the rest of creation. It's as if we, who are the firstfruits of redemption, are also experiencing the powers of the age to come in a way that is not yet available to the rest of creation.

This being subject to decay obviously affects Christian and non-Christian alike. Dr May raises a most interesting question when he postulates that being a Christian is no more likely to protect one from a 'flu epidemic than if one were a non-Christian. I myself find this a puzzle to which it may as yet be impossible to give definitive (*i.e.* statistically backed!) answers. What is clear to me is that there is much of the whole decaying process of the world from which we as Christians are most clearly delivered. Simple obedience to the Word of God will protect us from venereal disease because our life-style will not promote it. A love of God's Word will lead us to honour our bodies which are the temple of the Holy Spirit. This means that we are unlikely to smoke or drink excessively and so again, we find that we are protected from illnesses to which many non-Christians succumb. My own experience of much pastoral work within the church leads me to think that the prevalence of anxiety and depression within it is substantially different to that within the world at large. I do not mean to imply it is not there. Any pastor knows that it is, and in abundance. However, the answers are there as people move more into the peace and joy of Christ, and so they find their anxiety and depression lifting.

There are some very interesting but anecdotal, rather than statistically valid, accounts that can be gleaned from Christian writings as to the public health effects of local, powerful healing ministries. Approximately 250 years ago, in a district of Germany, a godly pastor by the name of Bloemheart took over the responsibility of the local parish church. Over the thirty years that he was in that district he exercised a powerful ministry of healing and casting out demons. It was said of that district that it enjoyed better health than any of the other districts in Germany.

Perhaps more verifiable in the modern scientific sense* are accounts of the life and ministry of such men as John G. Lake. This remarkable Christian business entrepreneur was called of God first to South Africa, where he established the rapidly growing and influential Apostolic faith churches, then later returned in the late 1920s to the state of Washington. Here, based in Spokane, he exercised a powerful healing ministry over a period of five years. It is recorded that 100,000 medically verified healings took place under his ministry during that five-year period. The Washington state Senior Public Health official commented that the health of the whole region had been affected by John G. Lake's ministry. It is at best speculation to state how this happened. Had the powers of darkness somehow been rolled back from a particular geographical location for a period of time? We may not yet see everything in the Spirit clearly, but we can certainly see some of the effects. Jesus himself, describing the work of the Holy Spirit, said that we may not see (or understand) all that he does, but we would certainly see his effects even as we see the effects of the wind in the trees (Jn. 3:8).

The principle of life working through death

2 Corinthians 4:12 tells us that 'Death is at work in us, but life is at work in you'. This very interesting passage seems to underline the pressures that all those in Christian leadership know are a part and parcel of our following the Lord Jesus Christ. Somehow the very pressures that we work under produce their own toll, whether that be at a mental, emotional, spiritual or physical level. It is into this context that Paul says, as quoted in Dr May's chapter, 'Though outwardly we are wasting away, yet inwardly we

* It is worth noting that science is not the ultimate arbiter of truth and nor is detailed statistical analysis, but rather what the Word of God says.

are being renewed day by day. For our light and momentary troubles are achieving for us an eternal glory that far outweighs them all. So we fix our eyes not on what is seen, but on what is unseen. For what is seen is temporary, but what is unseen is eternal' (2 Cor. 4:16). However this is certainly no willing surrender to increasing decay so much as joyful and obedient sacrifice for the sake of others. Earlier in this very passage, after Paul emphasizes that what is eternal is clearly more important than what is temporal, he tells us (4:11): 'We who are alive are always being given over to death for Jesus' sake, so that his life may be revealed in our mortal body'. It is the actual life of God which is finding expression, not just through our spiritual existence, but also our physical life. This was the great revelation that the founder of the Christian and Missionary Alliance, Dr A. B. Simpson, had when he himself was crippled through overwork and pulmonary disease. In his understanding that Christ was his life, he was able to take hold of healing. He worked from that day onwards with a renewed strength and vigour that had never been his even in his earliest days in the ministry when he was exceedingly fit. The subsequent tremendous growth of the Christian Alliance through the United States and across the world says volumes for this saintly man of God. Many other spiritual giants have emerged from this denomination that had its roots in A. B. Simpson's revelation of the glory and power of the risen Christ. The best known are F. F. Bosworth, who conducted massive healing crusades across the United States and Canada at the turn of the century, and A. W. Tozer, considered by many one of the most spiritual 'prophets' of recent years.

Unanswered questions

So why then do we go so often without this apparent 'liberty' that is available to the believer, *i.e.* the liberty of health and healing? It seems to me that there are a number of reasons that help to give us pointers in this area.

1. *The lies of Satan.* Satan is a liar and the father of lies. If there is some way that he can work out his task of

seeking to 'steal and kill and destroy', then he will do that. He will lie within our minds and within our bodies. Perhaps the greatest lie that he has perpetrated on the church is that Christ's salvation is really only effective for our spiritual needs. He has left us blind to the glorious truth that salvation is 'complete – spirit, soul and body, so that we may be preserved blameless'.

2. *The kingdom not yet fully realized.* It is not enough though just to say that Satan has kept God's people in bondage. I think we have to realize that we do now experience in only an incomplete and imperfect way the promise of the kingdom. We are still praying as our Lord taught us to pray, 'Thy will be done, on earth as it is in heaven'. That kingdom is neither fully realized nor perhaps even fully anticipated by us in this present age. It is this lack of faith that leads to the third area.

3. *Low level of faith and expectation in the church.* Lack of clear biblical teaching over many generations has led to the appalling low expectation of health and healing that is now experienced in the Body of Christ, the church. In addition modern scientific medicine has effectively become a religion of its own, with most of the church willingly bowing down at the altar of what the doctor says. There is little wonder that we see such lack of health in the church. The doctor has replaced the priest as the foremost prognosticator of future events. His 'divine' ability to give a prognosis has become a type of negative prophecy that usually inspires despair and fear in those who receive it. As believers we do not need to expect that the coming of illness will necessarily have a natural course and outcome. We live as believers not only within the natural realm but in the whole realm that is pervaded by the Spirit of God. When confronted with the reality ('fact') of sickness, we do not give in to the medical prognosis any more than we expect to give in to our feelings when we feel anxious, low or angry. Instead it is right at this point of vulnerability that we reach out to God in faith and take hold of the promises of his Word. We can challenge the powers of darkness in aggressive prayer that God will restore us to full health.

Seeing God at work in the physical

Tony Dale

My personal testimony of healing as a child. This began my search into the whole realm of healing · Creation was made perfect by God. Even Satan was beautiful before his fall · Pain, suffering, sickness and death are consequences of the fall of mankind. The work of Satan is the key factor in these consequences · God doesn't cause sickness. He is spoken of as the healer · Sin the cause of death and illness · Though God neither sends nor wills our illness and suffering he makes use of it · The attacks of Satan · Demonic possession · The 'fourth dimension' of the supernatural · An analogy from cancer of the destructive effects of life independent of God · Natural and supernatural healing · Christ is our life

Introduction

I can still remember the Friday when it began as clearly as yesterday. One of my older brothers was going out with a friend to play snooker, and I pleaded to go with him. However, they did not want younger brother tagging along! Anyway, I was feeling pretty grubby, and so had to stay at home. At one stage I spent time in bed, which during a holiday was most unlike me. I went to bed early, and woke up feeling quite a bit better. But by lunchtime I had to return from my normal Saturday swim, and collapsed in bed in a heap. By the evening, I was getting increasingly severe abdominal pains, and had begun vomiting.

The summer holidays were coming to an end, and in a

little over a week I would be going back for my last year at school. From my point of view being a missionary kid had far more compensations than problems. I loved our missionary school, and was deeply involved in all aspects of its life. I think it would be fair to say that I was a soccer fanatic, and knew that I would be going back as captain of the school team that year. It did not occur to me at this point that this presumably transitory illness would have any bearing on the excitement of heading back to school. But by the Sunday morning, I was as weak as a kitten, and still constantly vomiting. During the course of the night I had become deeply jaundiced. The pain had settled in the region of my liver.

Dad, who was working at the time as a doctor in Taipei, Taiwan, anticipating what was going on, had sent off some urine and blood tests the day before. I can still picture him coming in to see me in my bedroom after returning from church on the Sunday morning. 'Tony, I have the tests back now from the lab, and they show you have hepatitis. I am afraid it's likely to be quite a while before you are back properly on your feet. I would guess it will be a minimum of three months.'

My heart sank. A good friend of the family, another missionary, had just left staying with us. I recalled conversations with him. He was only just getting back on his feet following a severe bout of hepatitis. He had been unable to work for almost a year.

Although in the United Kingdom infectious hepatitis is not usually a desperately serious or life-threatening condition, that is by no means the case in Taiwan. Medical facilities in those days were far more primitive than they are now. By the Monday I was still vomiting profusely all the time, and already showing serious signs of weight loss and dehydration. My father decided to put up an intravenous drip to rehydrate me and feed me. He and my mum felt that it was best for them to look after me at home rather than put me in one of the hospitals where they would not have much confidence in the nursing and medical care given.

Monday through Wednesday are a blur in my mind. I

know that by Wednesday I had begun to look like just skin and bones. The vomiting seemed never to stop. When Mum washed me in the morning, and I had a chance to comb my hair, I saw how deeply jaundiced I looked. The whites of my eyes seemed almost orange. I was so weak I could not get out of bed to go to the toilet.

It was late on the Wednesday night when my mum came in to see me, having returned from our church prayer meeting. Pearl Young, a Pentecostal missionary friend, was with her. They came and sat down beside the bed, while Mum pulled out her Bible.

'We feel that the Lord Jesus wants us to pray for you, Tony. Is that all right?'

To be honest, I felt so sick I did not mind what they did. What was about to happen had little, if anything, to do with me.

My mum began to read from the last few verses of Mark's Gospel. 'These signs shall follow those who believe. They will lay hands on the sick, and they will recover.'

As they prayed, they laid hands on me. I do not remember feeling anything at all. Certainly there was no special manifestation of God's presence, as far as I could tell, in either the physical, emotional, or spiritual realm. It's just that I slept soundly all that night. The vomiting had stopped. And when I woke up in the morning, the jaundice was gone!

I was as weak as a kitten, but ravenously hungry. Over the next few days, I ate everything I could get my hands on. I remember clearly how at Friday lunchtime I was sitting up in bed tucking into the better part of half a roast chicken and roast potatoes. My dad wandered through from the clinic, and then called my mum.

'You can't possibly give him all this fatty food. Whatever is happening to him at the moment, his liver will have been absolutely flattened by the hepatitis. He can't cope with all these fancy things.'

Now, there is no doubt that my Dad was the head of the house. Although, as in any household, there were disagreements from time to time, it never even occurred to me to think anything but that Dad's word would hold. But this was one of those few occasions where Mum obviously felt she had to stand up to what he was saying. She challenged him that if Jesus had healed me, he would have done the job completely, and that I should be free to eat whatever I wanted. Since, by this stage, I had wolfed down most of the meal anyway, there seemed little point in Dad protesting further. There were no bad side-effects. By the following week, I was ready to head back to school. However, the school, having gathered that I had hepatitis, was most reluctant to let me back. Although hepatitis has a low infectivity, they did not want someone with what they assumed to be still active hepatitis taking part in school activities. For a frustrating two weeks, while I felt so well that I got myself into shape by practising football with our arch rivals, the Taipei American School, I had to put up with missing school. At the end of this time, it seemed ludicrous to keep me home any longer, and so the school relented.

Unknown to me, I had just begun my search into the whole realm of healing.

In the beginning

When God made the world, he repeatedly commented, 'And it was good'. The perfect creator God, in making a beautiful creation, made it perfectly. But any casual look, both at the world that we are a part of, and at people in particular, shows that this perfection has been marred. There is nothing in Genesis 1 or 2 to lead us to believe that pain and suffering, sickness or death, were intended by the Lord. But by the middle of Genesis 3 the whole situation has changed. Because of Adam and Eve's sin, we see God cursing the serpent, putting perpetual enmity between the serpent (Satan) and mankind, and warning Eve that the consequence of her sin is that child-bearing will now become a very painful experience. This is not to imply that before the fall, child-bearing might not have had some pain associated with it, in much the same way that if we fall over and cut ourselves it is painful. But this type of pain is not a negative thing, but rather the body reacting to pressures that would otherwise damage it. Even the ground becomes the recipient of God's curse, and man is from then on destined to have to toil very hard for his daily bread. Alongside this, he warned that from dust he came, and to dust he will return, *i.e.* his life is temporary because God is no longer going to allow him access to the tree of life.

Any attempt to understand the nature of sickness seems to me to be incomplete without reference to the work of Satan. Somehow, everything about his character is so malign and perverse that he has found the way to corrupt not only his own original beauty and perfection, but the beauty and perfection that God put within the world and within people.

In stark contrast to this, we see the majesty and splendour and purity of God. We cannot conceive of God being sick. Even the biblical accounts of God in the flesh give us no evidence that Jesus was ever sick. On the contrary, it is recognized prophetically of him (see Is. 53) that only when he suffered for us would it be necessary for him to 'be made sick' (v. 10 marginal reading).

The whole nature and character of God militates against his being involved in making people sick. To suggest that God makes people sick is, to my understanding of biblical principle, as contrary to his character as it is to suggest that he makes people sin. This is not to say that God cannot bring good out of evil. In all things our God 'works for the good to those who love him, who have been called according to his purpose' (Rom. 8:28). However, weaving the misshapen tapestries of our lives into a new and beautiful picture is hardly the same as saying he intended the discoloured and out-of-place threads in the first place.

The LORD, your healer

In the Old Testament, we see God revealing himself by a number of covenant names. One of the clearest indications we have of Jesus' divinity is his own clear identification of himself with the great 'I am' of the Old Testament. One of these marvellous covenant names by which God has chosen to show himself is 'I am the LORD, your healer' (Ex. 15:26 RSV). To my mind, this ties up with statements of the Lord Jesus, such as 'I have come that they may have life, and have it to the full' (Jn. 10:10), or 'In him was life, and that life was the light of men' (Jn. 1:4).

We know that God 'is light; in him there is no darkness at all' (1 Jn. 1:5). Can we conceive of there being anything unhealthy in God?

His nature, however, is not only revealed in that marvellous Old Testament covenant name, *Jehova Rapha*, but we see it beautifully lived out in the life of Jesus. From the earliest accounts in the gospels, we see the Lord going about 'throughout Galilee, teaching in their synagogues, preaching the good news of the kingdom, and healing every disease and sickness among the people. News about him spread all over Syria, and people brought to him all who were ill with various diseases, those suffering severe pain, the demon-possessed, the epileptics and the paralytics, and he healed them' (Mt. 4:23–24). Peter, in describing the life and work of the Lord Jesus to Cornelius, summarized his ministry by saying, 'You know . . . how God anointed Jesus of Nazareth with the Holy Spirit and power, and how he went around doing good and healing all who were under the power of the devil, because God was with him' (Acts 10:38).

Whether it is the desperately hoping, but doubting father with his epileptic son ('Lord, I believe; help my unbelief!'), or the pitiful leper ('Lord, if you will you can make me clean'), or the timid woman with the issue of blood, we see in each case the heart of God in action. When we behold his glory, full of grace and truth, we intuitively know that he wants to make us whole. His earthly ministry demonstrates this. His divinely revealed character demonstrates it. The gracious prompting and revealing of the Holy Spirit in our generation confirms his wish with mighty signs and wonders being reported from all over the world.

So why then does sickness or suffering in some form or other so often come into the believer's life? How do we understand verses such as, 'If you listen carefully to the voice of the LORD your God and do what is right in his eyes, if you pay attention to his commands and keep all his decrees, I will not bring on you any of the diseases I brought on the Egyptians' (Ex. 15:26)? Is it really God who inflicts us with sickness at times? How do we understand passages such as 1 Samuel 16:14 where it states, 'Now the Spirit of the Lord had departed from Saul, and an evil spirit from the Lord tormented him'?

To understand this type of statement we need to know something of the awesome sovereignty of God. God truly rules over all. Perhaps this can be understood more clearly in the light of the following story from Billy Bray's life, that rough-hewn Cornish coal miner whom God used to bring multitudes to faith.

The village butcher, a foul-mouthed and evil-tempered man with many evil ways, had a long-standing antagonism to Billy and his preaching. One day the butcher, whose shop was near Billy's little cottage, overheard Billy praying in his characteristically noisy fashion, pleading with God to provide his needed food. The butcher, thinking to make fun of Billy, grabbed some meat and threw it in to Billy through his window, shouting, 'Satan's brought your meat, Billy.' Billy is said to have immediately retorted, 'Satan's brought it but God sent it!'

The author of life

God is the author of life. It is inconceivable that he who brings life would also seek to destroy us with death. But the unchangeable sovereign God has established immutable laws both physical and spiritual in his universe. That is as true now as it was in the Garden of Eden and as it was when Paul penned the words, 'the wages of sin is death' (Rom. 6:23). It is naïve in the extreme to extrapolate from this that any given sin necessarily leads to a specific sickness. That this may be the case on some occasions is not doubted, but that certainly does not seem to be the general rule. However, in principle behind the whole puzzle of sickness is the mystery of sin and the authority that is allowed to Satan and his minions by the sovereign Lord.

Clearly since the fall man's days have been numbered. But biblically it seems that the reduction in lifespan from the hundreds of years that people such as Methuselah and Enoch enjoyed to our present allotted three score and ten came about not because of inherent physical weakness in the bodies God had created for us, but because of the increasing and cumulative effect of sin. God, seeing that people's days were filled with evil, sovereignly decided to limit our lives to a length of time in which we could respond to him but would not be able to perpetuate ever-increasing wickedness.

This naturally raises certain questions as to the aging process. It is a clear fact of life that as our bodies get older they become weaker. But this is not a *prima facie* evidence that God intended it to be so. Is this not an extension of the underlying principle that the wages of sin is death? And does not God command us in his Word to seek to overcome in every area of our lives, including in areas of physical weakness? It was said of Moses when he died at 120 years of age that 'his eyes were not weak nor his strength gone' (Dt. 34:7). Even Jesus was not killed by the suffering of the cross, by the sin and sickness of the world that he bore or by the spear that was thrust into his side, but rather he gave up his own life. He had earlier said of his death, 'The reason my father loves me is that I lay down my life – only to take it up again. No-one takes it from me, but I lay it down of my own accord. I have authority to lay it down and authority to take it up again' (Jn. 10:17–18a).

Does this mean, then, that we can expect to go into old age even as Moses did with our eyesight intact (not needing glasses!) and our hearing still as youthful as ever? Is it taking the passage too literally to believe from 1 Thessalonians 5:23 that God really does intend to preserve complete 'your whole spirit, soul and body' at the coming of our Lord Jesus Christ? I find these very difficult questions to answer. It seems to me that God holds out as a genuine possibility that the sanctifying work of his Holy

Spirit can work in us so completely that we are brought in increasing measure into wholeness whether spiritually, in the realm of our soul, or in relation to our physical body. Romans 8:11 makes it clear that 'he who raised Christ from the dead will also give life to your mortal bodies through his Spirit, who lives in you'.

A. B. Simpson, the founder of the Christian and Missionary Alliance group of churches, certainly understood these scriptures in this fashion. In a beautiful tract he wrote entitled *Himself*, he tells how he came to realize that Paul literally meant it when he says in Galatians 2:20, 'The life I live in the body, I live by faith in the Son of God, who loved me and gave himself for me.'

Just as on this side of eternity it seems that we do not reach sinless perfection, although this is clearly our goal and desire, so it appears to me that for most of us, our physical 'completeness' remains something that we reach out to God for though we may not necessarily experience it in its fullness. As our individual faith grows, and as the faith of Christ's church locally and worldwide grows, so we are more likely to see these manifestations of God's glorious and full salvation.

God's use of suffering

Although it is clear that God neither wills, nor in our usual sense of the word sends, sickness or suffering our way, it is equally clear from Scripture that he actively uses them. How are we to understand this?

David du Plessis tells the following story. He was busily involved in organizing the first international, ecumenical, charismatic conference. Many thousands of delegates were expected from all around the world. With just a few months to go he was involved in a serious accident and was effectively moved out of the way 'by God' to spend the final months up to the conference in a hospital bed. From here he had to let go totally of the conference and watch helplessly while others took it on. As he waited on God he discovered that although this may have been an accident from a human perspective, God was certainly using it to deal with many things in his own character.

Dr Paul Yonggi Cho of Full Gospel Central Church in Seoul, South Korea, is another man who has learnt much through suffering. His church has also been privileged to see what is probably the most phenomenal growth of any church ever. The endless signs and wonders and miracles of healing that his congregation experiences have to be seen to be believed. And if my experience of going out there to witness these things is anything to go by, even seeing still leaves a certain amount of disbelief with our sceptical western mind-set!

In the early days of his ministry he suffered for ten years from a severe heart condition. Often it was all he could do to stand up and preach. At times he could only stand if others supported him. Sometimes he would be in bed for weeks unable to fulfil any of his normal commitments. During this time God taught him many things. He realized that if the church was to grow beyond his capacity as an individual leader, he would have to learn to delegate. It was out of this that his home cell system began which has subsequently been of tremendous blessing not only in his own church, but through his life and teaching in multitudes of churches across the world. Out of this suffering came his own deep dependence on God. Out of the poverty of these years came an unswerving confidence that God was able to supply his needs. With endless hours to wait on God he was able to learn to put his confidence entirely in the Word of God. He began to see that, irrespective of his circumstances or physical condition, the Word of God was true. God had promised him abundant life, blessings and health and he would hold on to God until he saw his promises fulfilled. This was not in the nice comfy affluence of our western society but rather in the extremely poor reconstruction period Korea went through following the Korean War.

God uses suffering and sickness. God is often mightily glorified in our lives through the lessons we learn in these dark times. For many of us it would be true to say that we learn far more in times of suffering and pressure than we do when all is going well. But we would be robbing

God of even greater glory if we doubted that he is not more mightily glorified when we are subsequently delivered from all of our distresses. As the Psalmist says,

> He forgives all my sins
>   and heals all my diseases;
> he redeems my life from the
>   pit
>   and crowns me with love
>   and compassion.
> He satisfies my desires with
>   good things,
>   so that my youth is renewed
>   like the eagle's.

(Ps. 103:3–5)

Satan's strategies

It would now be appropriate to try to examine a little more clearly the mechanisms whereby Satan seems able to attack us. The explosion of interest in the occult in our western societies over the past few decades has highlighted for true Christians the reality of the spirit world. Many had not only been very unaware of the work of the Holy Spirit, but had also been if anything even more ignorant of the work of the evil one. Passages such as Ephesians 6 that told us that 'our struggle is not against flesh and blood, but against the rulers, against the powers of this dark world and against the spiritual forces of evil in the heavenly realms', although well known, were to most of us closer to figments of our imagination than true descriptions of our experience of prayer. However, the last twenty years have seen all of that change dramatically.

A number of years ago I was invited up to the newly opened Jesus Centre in city centre Birmingham by Nick Cuthbert. The meeting had progressed through a time of worship and praise and Nick was about to introduce me as the speaker. All of a sudden there was an awful commotion outside the main door of the meeting hall. I went out to see what was happening. To my surprise and consternation there was a young man having an epileptic fit.

I had only just started my clinical training at medical school and had had no exposure to this before. I was not sure what to do, but fortunately by this time Nick had come out to join me. I have no idea who was leading the meeting at this point!

The lad came round from his fit fairly quickly and we began to ask him some questions. The story came out roughly as follows. He had been released from a mental hospital earlier in the day. He had been walking past the place where the meeting was in progress when he felt a strong urge to come inside. He had followed the sound of the singing and was about to enter the meeting room through the door when he had the epileptic fit. Although he was on treatment for a chronic mental disorder (schizo-phrenia), so far as I know he had not previously been diagnosed as epileptic. There was something about his story that did not sound desperately medical to either of us. We told him that we would be happy to pray with him and ask Jesus to touch him. He gladly consented. But as soon as we prayed he had another fit.

By now we were convinced that we were dealing with something demonic. We questioned him a little bit more regarding his condition and together challenged this evil spirit in the name of Jesus to leave him. After a brief period of hysterics (*i.e.* the evil spirit causing more fitting and trying to scare us all off) the spirit left him and he was set free.

On another occasion, after I had been practising medi-cine for a number of years in the East End of London, a West Indian lady walked into the surgery to see me. She normally saw one of my partners, but on this occasion I was covering for his surgery. She had just come in for a routine repeat of some tranquillizers that she was on, but as she was chatting away to me while I wrote out the prescription she mentioned something that made me sit up and take notice.

'Doctor, I have begun to hear voices. Can you tell me what is happening?'

Could I tell her what was happening! When that sort of comment is made to you, you learn to take it seriously. Immediately it seemed as if my mind was racing in two contradictory directions. Medically speaking I know that delusions and hearing voices are quite strongly suggestive of a schizophrenic-type illness. Should I be pursuing further questions along this line and seeing if there were other thought disorders?

However, I was also saying to myself, 'This sounds demonic.' I had had enough experience of this by now to know that demons can attack people's minds in this way. In a brief examination, with many other patients waiting outside the surgery also needing to be heard, there is not a lot of time to pursue lengthy discussions. Rightly or wrongly I opted for the second line of questioning.

'Do you think these voices could have any spiritual significance?' I asked her. Her immediate response to this was to state that she thought the problem was demonic!! This rather made me sit up. Further questioning did not show any clear connection with the occult. But since she was clear in her own mind that this was something evil and that was also the witness I felt within my own spirit, I told her I would happily pray for her. I prayed very simply in the name of Jesus and commanded the spirit to let go of its hold on her mind. I then also shared with her a little more of the love of Jesus and helped her to give her life to the Lord. When I saw her again in the surgery about six months later, she was really pleased to tell me that the voices had never returned.

The story however has some interesting sequelae. Her daughter came in to see me sometime after that. I did not know the family well and did not realize that the girl I was seeing was her daughter. She had come in complaining of a recurrence of a severe lower abdominal pain. In looking at the notes I saw that she had been treated on a number of occasions for chronic pelvic inflammatory disease. Examination confirmed that this was again the most likely diagnosis and I offered to start her on a course of antibiotics. At this point she mentioned to me that she had noticed a real change in her mother since I had prayed for her. This gave me the chance to talk about spiritual things. I explained to her that her pelvic inflammatory disease was a direct result of the promiscuous life-style she had been living. As we talked around this I had a growing conviction that she was reaping in her own body the literal fruit of the scriptural statement: 'the wages of sin is death' (Rom. 6:23). I explained to her how the enemy capitalizes on sin in our lives and uses it as a means of subjecting us to his challenge. Now I am, of course, aware as a physician that at a physical level, in this type of condition we can take a high vaginal swab and probably culture certain organisms. I also know that chronic pelvic inflammatory disease from a medical point of view is associated with infection by pathogenic organisms around the fallopian tubes and in the uterine support ligaments. But what the Lord was telling me was that the problem was not primarily physical but spiritual. I explained this to the young girl and then offered to pray for her. As I laid hands on her and rebuked the condition the pain immediately subsided.

I would love to be able to tell you that she subsequently became a Christian and that everything in the garden was rosy. However, that was not the case. She steadfastly resisted all the rest that I shared with her, both on that and on subsequent occasions as I urged her to leave her damaging life-style and hand her life over to the Lord. Interestingly enough though, in spite of her unwillingness to respond to the Lord's claims, she had no further recurrence of the pain and other symptoms of her condition during the time that I was looking after her. I last heard from her about a year after the incidents I have described above and she still seemed to be physically fine.

Healing of unbelievers

This story raises another very interesting area. The experience of many people in the healing ministry around the world seems to show that it is often easier for an unbeliever to receive healing than a believer. Again I cannot fully explain this phenomenon. However I do see pointers in Scripture which help us to understand this difficulty.

Jesus unashamedly worked in the supernatural power of God to bring healing to vast numbers of people. In doing this he was both demonstrably attacking Satan's domain and giving a signpost to the healed, and to those who knew that the kingdom of God was at hand. Scripture is quite plain that seeing a miracle does not make a believer. In John 12:37 it says, 'Even after Jesus had done all these miraculous signs in their presence, they still would not believe in him.' Yet, the very fact that a supernatural healing or other miracle had taken place, was an indictment against them. Earlier in the same gospel, Jesus could say to another crowd, 'Do not believe me unless I do what my Father does. But if I do it, even though you do not believe me, believe the miracles, that you may learn and understand that the Father is in me, and I in the Father' (Jn. 10:37–38). Miracles did point people clearly to Jesus. However to become a true believer has such startling moral implications that many prefer to exchange the obvious truth of what they see (whether in the miraculous or in nature) for a lie, so that they can continue in their life-style that takes them away from God.*

My own limited experience confirms what many from this country and abroad have experienced. Many times in praying for unbelievers in the surgery, I have seen God graciously and miraculously touch them in physical, emotional, mental, or spiritual ways. Alongside this, I think of many with physical conditions that I have prayed for within a church context, for whom there has been little discernible improvement. It is interesting that in my case, whereas I would nearly always have faith to see the Lord set people free from emotional or mental distress, I do not yet move with the same confidence in the physical realm.

Whether the healing experienced by the unbeliever is in the same order as that experienced by the believer, I do not know. To me it is clear that the believer has a right to approach his Heavenly Father for the 'children's bread.' (See Mark 7, where Jesus heals the Syro-Phoenician's

---

* See Romans 1:18–32 for a further biblical exposition of this theme.

daughter, for the context of this expression.) Our healing as believers flows from the atoning work of Christ. Matthew makes this clear by quoting a passage from Isaiah 53 in the context of Jesus healing all those who came to him. Whereas the Old Testament Hebrew words for griefs, sicknesses, sorrows and pains are interchangeable, in Matthew 8 it is the more precise Greek wording that we have. Here it plainly says of Jesus that he did his healings in order 'to fulfil what was spoken through the prophet Isaiah: "He took up our infirmities and carried our diseases." '

The application of this scripture to the crowds coming to Jesus seems to show that potentially Christ's salvation, as including our physical needs, could reach out to all mankind, even as his coming to save us from our sins is a gift that God makes freely available to all. In both situations it is equally clear that not all will avail themselves of God's gift.

The unseen world

It is important that we recognize that the realm of the spirit pervades, and in a sense supersedes, the natural realms that we see and perceive with our senses. Paul describes this situation by saying that that which we see is temporal while that which we do not see is eternal. It is almost as if he is saying that the unseen world is the more real. I suspect, from the Lord's perspective, that this is absolutely true! But of course the unseen realm does not just include God, the Holy Spirit and all of his angelic hosts. We are aware that Scripture teaches that a third of the angelic hosts fell along with Satan. Dr Paul Yonggi Cho, in describing this whole realm of the spirit, took up the very useful phrase, 'the fourth dimension'. The natural realms ('dimensions') of the physical world are contained within, and controlled by, the larger and vastly more powerful spiritual realms – *i.e.* the fourth dimension. If we do not understand this then we are not only going to fail to understand the workings of God. We will also be baffled as to how it is possible for occult powers and religions also at times to work miracles.*

I grew up as a child with missionary parents who were working in Taiwan. There was an annual festival in the south of the island where the local priests worked themselves up into a real frenzy on the idols' feast day. In this 'demonized' state they were able to walk on hot coals, slash themselves with knives, and let others beat them viciously with sticks, apparently without suffering pain or other physical sequelae. I actually have some photographs that were taken of this happening. This was not mere manipulation but a manifestation of demonic protection.

The language of Jesus in 'rebuking the storm' that was seeking to engulf the boat in which he and his disciples were travelling shows that on that occasion he perceived even the weather as being controlled by spiritual forces.

I think the above comments and anecdotes serve to illustrate a point that C. S. Lewis made once in his introduction to his well-known book *The Screwtape Letters*: 'There are two equal and opposite errors into which our race can fall about the devils. One is to disbelieve in their existence. The other is to believe and to feel an excessive and unhealthy interest in them. They themselves are equally pleased by both errors and hail a materialist or a magician with the same delight.'

In my own admittedly somewhat limited experience, I have seen people with epilepsy, schizophrenia, severe headaches, phobias, severe chest pain or abdominal pain, various obsessive compulsive disorders, and various forms of depression, all set free from their conditions by a simple word of command to an underlying spirit. I think it would be equally true to say that I have also seen most of the same conditions where the cause did not appear to be something demonic but had a much more physical or circumstantial explanation.

To try and identify all illness – whether physical or emotional/mental conditions – as being directly caused by a specific demonic entity is, I think, rather naïve and quite

* To study this area, read Dr Cho's excellent book *The Fourth Dimension* (Logos International).

inaccurate. However, to deny the reality that often this may be the case is equally foolish. In fact, it is to deny people the very real opportunity of release which would be theirs in the name of Jesus.

The image of cancer

I think this would be an appropriate place to make some brief comments on the nature of malignant (cancerous) conditions. Increasing medical understanding is giving us a clearer idea of the physical, chemical and mental antecedents to cancer. It must be remembered that the disease is not one condition but a generic term that applies to a vast number of totally different complaints. However, there seem to be some unifying factors between the malignancies. It appears as if the rapidly dividing malignant cells have a 'life force' of their own. This is a destructive force which is seeking to overcome the normal cells by which its cells are surrounded. Not only can these cells grow and divide and squeeze out the life of cells around them, but in many of the more highly malignant conditions little clumps of these cells can break off the main tumour and travel via the blood stream or the lymphatics to be deposited in new locations. Here they can effectively attach themselves as parasites and again begin multiplying. These are the 'secondaries' that one talks about in a patient with cancer.

The nature of this 'independent' life that is so destructive seems akin to Jesus' comment on Satan's work in John 10:10, 'The thief comes only to steal and kill and destroy'. The very word 'malignant' is derived from the same Latin word that we use for malign or evil. I have no way of proving this, but my impression is that malignancies probably have a demonic component that is somehow energizing the destructive process.

What is clear as we look at the ministry of Jesus is that he feared neither demons nor disease. Whether he rebuked a fever or applied a mud poultice to a blind man's eyes, or just 'spoke the word', he seemed to have complete confidence that healing would result. His own intimate walk with his Father meant that from his place of close communion he only involved himself in doing 'what he saw his Father doing'.

Healing

So what is happening when we experience healing? It is quite plain that the Lord has so designed our bodies that they naturally tend to heal themselves. From a physiological point of view it is beautiful to see the way that a broken bone can, with such intricacy, both knit itself back together and be remodelled to its original shape and strength. In differing circumstances where the body is invaded by pathogenic organisms, our natural immune systems (unless knocked out by some pathological process such as AIDS) swing into action and immediately attack, and if given the time overwhelm the offending pathogen. Is this process analogous to biblical divine healing?

My own opinion is that it is not. This natural healing power that the Lord has placed in the body is to me an example of his wonderful grace flowing to the just and the unjust. This is quite different from the specific manifestation and impartation of life that is offered to the believer. The great mystery and promise of the New Testament is that of 'Christ in you, the hope of glory'. God is not offering us some discreet package apart from himself when he offers to heal us. He is in effect continuing that great transaction whereby his life is substituted for our life. The apostle Paul when talking about this could say, 'The life I live in the body, I live by faith in the Son of God, who loved me and gave himself for me' (Gal. 2:20). Similarly in another place he says, 'If the Spirit of him who raised Jesus from the dead is living in you, he who raised Christ from the dead will also give life to your *mortal* bodies through his Spirit, who lives in you' (Rom. 8:11).

Oral Roberts is a remarkable American healing evangelist, whose crusades around the world have seen somewhere in the region of five million people give their lives to Christ, of whom approximately one million would also claim to have been physically healed. He views the relationship between the natural and the supernatural as two streams from the same healing Lord. His commitment to natural methods such as sensible diet and adequate exercise is evidenced by his having established a large and fully accredited medical school within the heart of his university complex in Tulsa, Oklahoma. Symbolically flowing from one fountain at the front of the hospital complex is a stream which divides into two tributaries, the stream of prayer and supernatural healing and the stream of medical care.

When a patient comes to see me as a doctor to have help or advice as to how they may be made well, they are, in a genuine sense, co-operating with the already revealed will of God. God desires our health. God has not limited us to purely natural means. In fact for the believer, as opposed to the unbeliever, he has actually given clear instructions as to what we should do when we are ill.

> Is any one of you in trouble? He should pray. Is anyone happy? Let him sing songs of praise. Is any one of you sick? He should call the elders of the church to pray over him and anoint him with oil in the name of the Lord. And the prayer offered in faith will make the sick person well; the Lord will raise him up. If he has sinned, he will be forgiven. There-fore confess your sins to each other and pray for each other so that you may be healed (Jas. 5:13–16).

It is astounding to me that such a clear command of Scripture can be so flagrantly disobeyed by large segments of Christ's church. Our first recourse when ill is prayer. If we find that our own praying seems inadequate then we should be calling for the leaders of our church to stand with us in prayer. In Ezekiel 34 the shepherds of Israel are castigated prophetically by the Lord for their lack of interest in this area. 'You have not strengthened the weak or healed the sick or bound up the injured' (Ezk. 34:4a).

How could God so severely reprimand them for something that they had no power to do? The truth of the matter is that this power had already been delegated to them by the Lord. Similarly today church leadership should be actively encouraging God's people to reach out to him for healing. This will include medical means where appropriate, but foundational and preceding our desire for medical means should be our reaching to God for his active and compassionate involvement in our needs.

There is much mystery in this whole realm of suffering and pain as well as sickness. There are many questions to which I still have no answers. I know that of the many with whom I pray only some are clearly and dramatically healed. Another small proportion are obviously touched and restored at a spiritual level even while their physical needs apparently remain unmet. This still leaves a number who are not apparently helped in any obvious way. Does this mean that we stop praying? Would we stop witnessing to people just because all of them do not immediately respond to the Lord Jesus? Do we stop praying for God's answers in other areas of our lives because we do not receive the answer on the first request?

What we do see is that God's wonderful salvation is very much more extensive than most of us had initially realized. As we explore the wonders of God's grace and learn to reach out ourselves with increasing confidence in his word and faith in his ability, so we see the Lord working among us more and more. There is an enemy which the Bible tells us will not be overcome in this age. That enemy is death. Unless Jesus returns first, we will all walk through that particular gateway. However even death has been 'swallowed up in victory. "Where, O death, is your victory? Where, O death, is your sting?" ' (1 Cor. 15:54–55). The Bible does not teach us that we must effectively become more and more decrepid and racked by disease until we die. We are encouraged to reach out and expect his life and strength until our earthly ministry is complete. At this point each one of us will have to lay down our life.

The wonder of the redemption bought for us at Calvary is that Christ offers us himself. Not only does Scripture teach that he is 'our righteousness, sanctification, and redemption', but also that he is 'our life'. In a wonderful way beyond anything that we can adequately understand or explain, when Jesus died on the cross, he not only carried the full weight of our sin, but also of our suffering, pain and sickness.

Response to Tony Dale

Peter May

Our debate focuses onto three distinct areas:

1. the definition of miracle
2. the teaching of the New Testament
3. the medical evidence.

1. Concerning definitions, Tony Dale does not commit himself to precisely what he means by the term 'miracle'. An influential book* recently written by another doctor uses this definition: 'the healing of organic disease by a means or at a speed, inexplicable medically and preceded by prayer in the name of Jesus Christ'. Certainly in those terms I would admit to having seen several miracles and affirm that whilst they are unusual they are not all that uncommon. I am not contending that God doesn't answer our prayers in often inexplicable and quite striking ways. However, I am contending that the miracles of Christ are of a different order. While I do not believe we can satisfactorily define a miracle, I want to restrict the use of the term to describe healings that closely resemble those of Christ – instantaneous, complete healings, at a word, perhaps at a distance, with no relapse and including *every*

* Dr Rex Gardner, *Healing Miracles* (Darton, Longman and Todd, 1986), p. 1.

kind of disease. To use the word 'miracle' in this restricted sense is not some petty point in order to win an argument. It is to help us see things that differ, to retain our wonder at the miracles of Christ and to help us think more clearly as to what we can expect today.

The miracles of Christ are of a totally different order from anything I have ever come across. It is often said by non-medical people that Christ's healings were usually of a psychosomatic type. They were not. If for the sake of argument you put to one side the cases of demon possession, nearly all the remaining miracles were of a frankly physical type most of which are still *incurable* today – scoliosis, the withered hand, congenital blindness, deafness with mutism, epilepsy, leprosy, paralysis and of course death itself.

2. Concerning the New Testament evidence, Tony Dale rests heavily on a view of the atonement that includes physical healing as well as forgiveness in its achievements. I agree with him that this is a key issue and needs to be faced squarely. I refer the reader back to my earlier comments on the matter (p. 38). That the death of Christ was a penalty paid for our sins, we both agree. In what sense however can Christ's death be a penalty paid for our sicknesses? In what sense can our sicknesses deserve death? John Stott has written, 'So to speak of Christ atoning for our sicknesses is to mix categories; it is not an intelligible notion.'*

3. Medically Tony claims miracles are happening all over the world and rests heavily on anecdotes to support this. Over the past twenty years I have heard many of these stories. They are impressive in the many books that proliferate (and even repeat the same examples). They are even more moving when heard from the lips of a powerful orator – many of whom travel extensively telling their glad tidings to eager audiences.

However when one asks critical questions and pursues hard data, my experience is that the edifice invariably

* J. R. W. Stott, *The Cross of Christ* (IVP, 1986), p. 245.

collapses. I have referred to the well-known evangelist who claimed in Southampton to have healed a boy of Down's Syndrome. Subsequent correspondence revealed that the boy was not a mongol at all and is still mentally retarded. A best-selling writer has written of a child he healed of deafness and severe brain damage. Describing it as 'perhaps the most remarkable healing that took place in the life of a child', he wrote that the child was 'almost a human vegetable' and that medically there was no hope of improvement. I now have a copy of the consultant's letter. He stated emphatically that he did not think the child was deaf but 'somewhat behind' in his development at fifteen months and that time alone would show how well he would do. Another famous healer has written of a man he healed of blindness from diabetic retinopathy. It appears that the man is now lost without trace. A girl who claimed healing of diabetes at a university mission meeting had sugar in her urine the next morning.

A psychiatrist who claimed healing of a peptic ulcer had four days earlier had a normal gastroscopy! A girl who told her GP that she had been healed of a heart murmur at a meeting of her house church had to come to terms with the fact that her murmur was louder than ever. A claim in the Christian press to the healing of a throat tumour was found to have resulted from a misunderstanding of an ambiguous X-ray report. The doctor confirmed that the man was still having treatment for his underlying condition which was unchanged. 'One would find it very difficult to support any claim of miraculous healing,' he wrote.

Nine years after the event, a vicar claimed to have healed a man of 'terminal renal disease'. Subsequently he had to admit to his congregation that he had seriously misunderstood the nature of the illness. He had not attempted to check his facts and the reality was far more complicated than he had imagined. Nor could he have been expected to have understood the disease and its effects. The original illness was tuberculosis which resulted in renal damage, stone formation, high blood pressure and recurrent urine infections. The 'laying on of hands' occurred during one of these many urine infections. Fortunately the patient also had the good sense to take antibiotics and when he next saw his consultant he was told his urine was 'clear' (*i.e.* not currently infected). The vicar assumed too much! The man's life had not been at risk since he had active T.B. some thirty years ago which was then treated successfully with drugs. To this day he has kidney stones, takes daily treatment for his blood pressure, and the week after the claim was made went down with a further urine infection!

An interesting case came to light during an inquiry into evidences of miraculous healing conducted by members of the Christian Medical Fellowship in the mid-1970s and was presented as the most remarkable story to be unearthed by their investigation. The case was subsequently described in the *British Medical Journal* of 24 December 1983. The author of that article, Dr Rex Gardner, repeated his account of it in his book *Healing Miracles* (see p. 10), and other accounts of it are to be found elsewhere.* It concerns the healing of a chronic varicose ulcer on a lady's leg in the early 1970s. It seems the best that can be said for this case is that a longstanding venous ulcer improved dramatically over a period of at least a week, during which time specific prayer was made for its healing on two occasions.

Now it may be that something unusual happened here and certainly all those involved, not least the patient, were right to thank God for his goodness. Their prayers were certainly answered. Fifteen years after the event, Dr Gardner feels able to cite it in his book on miracles as his leading example. But it has to be said that the healing was not instantaneous, requiring two prayer meetings a week apart. Nor was any astonishing event actually *observed* — for the ulcer remained bandaged on each occasion. Furthermore, it is a well-documented medical phenom-

---

* Edmunds and Scorer, *Some Thoughts on Faith Healing* (Christian Medical Fellowship, 1979, 3rd ed.), p. 69.
Bridge and Phypers, *More Than Tongues Can Tell* (Hodder and Stoughton, 1982), pp. 35ff.
Donald Bridge, *Signs And Wonders Today* (IVP, 1985), p. 164.

enon that chronic venous ulcers if cleaned, bandaged and elevated can heal dramatically over a period of a week. Indeed I have seen it happen to one of my patients just recently.

In contrast, the immediate, complete healings of Christ were performed in full view of sceptical onlookers who were filled with amazement and said, 'We have never seen anything like this!' (Mk. 2:12).

The real significance of this case is to my mind not so much that it is somewhat unremarkable in itself, but that it continues so many years later to be offered as a significant, contemporary example of miraculous healing. One account (*More Than Tongues Can Tell*) says that it 'is typical of hundreds which have come out of the charismatic movement over the last twenty years'. I submit that if actual miracles were happening in this country on a fraction of the scale that is claimed, then this case would long ago have been surpassed and faded into oblivion.

Is it too much to ask after twenty years of inquiry for me to find *one claim* to such frankly physical miraculous healing which can be validated?

Tony Dale, like every other healer I have questioned, admits to having less confidence about praying for *physical* healing. Many of the claims made (and I include the claims made by Tony Dale) do not lend themselves to objective assessment. Whilst not denying that his jaundice settled remarkably, early memories from childhood of around thirty years ago are difficult to evaluate in the absence of blood reports of bilirubin and other liver function tests taken immediately before and after the prayer meeting.

Dr Dale gives us only two other examples of physical healing from his own experience. Concerning the boy outside the youth club, most epileptics are unable to hold a meaningful conversation immediately after a Grand-Mal fit. Usually they go into a deep sleep. He says they witnessed a period of hysterics and I would suggest that that is where the diagnosis lay. If he was set free from his 'fits', what about his more serious schizophrenia? Did God not heal that as well, and if not, why not? Unfortunately there is no reported follow-up. I suspect also that lack of continuing contact is the reason why non-believers appear to be healed more often than believers. It would also explain why peripatetic healers claim more sensational wonders than local ministers who have to live with their results! As for the girl with pains attributed to pelvic inflammatory disease, subjective symptoms by their nature cannot be objectively assessed. Laparoscopic examinations before and after would have enabled doctors to observe any change in her pelvic organs, but we do not have this information.

To learn that Oral Roberts has brought physical healing to one million people doesn't fill me with any confidence. One valid example would be worth a great deal. The man in the gospel story who had a withered hand must have had an interrupted nerve supply, wasted muscles and seized-up joints. In an instant and at a word of command, without even the laying on of hands, we are told in effect that the nerves became intact, the muscle bulk was restored and the joints moved freely. Any doctor seeing that today would be shocked to his boots! The story would be headline news. Just think of the fuss they made over Uri Geller when he appeared to bend a fork!

There is a whole wealth of illnesses that can be easily assessed – broken and severed limbs, congenital abnormalities, insulin-dependent diabetes, emphysema, AIDS syndrome, leprosy, hemiplegia, cystic fibrosis, muscular dystrophy, *etc. etc.* What is Tony saying about cancer? Is this disease particularly satanic or does it distress him because it repeatedly calls the lie to the whole signs and wonders movement and reduces it to the level of trivia? Recoveries from secondary spread of cancer do occur but are very rare and Christians do not seem to be seeing the phenomenon any more frequently than anyone else.

The idea of dying a healthy death in old age is very odd. I can imagine it might sound more reasonable to young people, but I wonder what older readers who can no longer run as fast as they used to, will make of it?

This whole debate then is about truth – the truth of the theology of the New Testament and the truth concerning the medical facts. The average reader will find it easier to assess the weight of the New Testament evidence which he can study for himself. The medical data however are often inaccessible and all too often claims by doctors themselves confuse the issues! In my experience the worst offenders are those doctors who specialize in one area and then make medical claims about cases outside their normal professional experience.

The issues before us have enormous implications. Are we commanded to go into all the world and miraculously heal the sick? Should we be encouraging church leaders to shift their emphasis from evangelism to healing? Should we allow people's assurance of forgiveness to be undermined because they remain physically unwell? What has this movement with its peripatetic wonder-workers got to contribute to Christian caring for the chronic sick? What are we to make of the growing triumphalism and prosperity movement offering health and wealth for all in today's church? Should we raise the church's expectations to see as regular events the sort of miracles which if they happen at all today are an incredibly rare phenomenon? Will repeated false claims eventually discredit and publicly undermine the whole evangelical cause?

When the Israelites arrived in the Promised Land, they ate bread and grain. We are told, 'The manna stopped the day after they ate this food from the land; there was no longer any manna for the Israelites, but that year they ate of the produce of Canaan' (Jos. 5:12). Their time in the wilderness had been accompanied by exceptional provision in exceptional circumstances. God could have provided supernatural manna to the present day. However he did not. They had to get on with the humdrum business of digging the ground, sowing the seeds, awaiting the harvests, and experiencing droughts and famines.

Similarly, supernatural healing could be part of God's normal provision for us today, but I submit that plainly it is not. We must face up to the hard facts of reality. The truth of these matters – medically, pastorally and evangelistically – is of vital concern to us all.

Part 2
Healing and miracle

Roger Cowley and Bill Lees

An invitation to expectancy

Hesitations about expectancy

An invitation to expectancy

Roger Cowley

This essay has a personal note: through John Wimber and others, the author's position has recently changed regarding signs and wonders · The word 'miracle' is difficult to define because of presuppositions. It is best avoided in favour of 'signs' and 'wonders' · It is the author's belief that God acted through Jesus Christ to bring healing, and that he gives power and authority to his disciples today to heal; such healing may be termed 'miraculous' in the sense of being a wonderful sign of God's activity · Nine points of probable agreement among Christians

My attitudes to healing and 'miracle' have changed recently, though my basic beliefs have not, so far as I can tell. First I shall set out some aspects of what I believe, and secondly I shall try to show how my expectancy and practice have altered. Readers who want to know my background at the outset may like to read the two parts in reverse order.

'Miracle' in English

Television interviewer: 'Are you planning to meet the
    South Sudanese leader?'
Mother Theresa: 'I'm praying for it.'
Interviewer: 'So you think there's a chance?'
Mother Theresa: 'With God all things are possible.'

Here are two people who are, in fact, speaking different languages! Mother Theresa believes in the power of prayer and the sovereignty of God. The television interviewer appears to view prayer as something that just might help, given a bit of luck.

Recently I led a home group discussion on the meaning of 'miracle'. We failed to come up with any working definition, and the conversation illustrated the way that the word has come to be used very loosely in English. It is often applied to improbable and infrequent events, occurrences of unknown explanation, and remarkable and wonderful happenings. This sort of usage is not likely to take us very far in either philosophy or theology.

Attempts to define 'miracle' mostly concentrate either on the nature of miracle, or on its results. 'A miracle is a violation of the laws of nature' is an example of the first type of definition. 'A miracle is something that creates faith, or excites wonder' is an example of the second. 'An event inexplicable by natural laws and so ascribed to divine or supernatural action' (*Penguin English Dictionary*) combines the two types.

Such definitions raise many problems. 'Natural laws' are statements of observed regularities in nature. They are not explanations of why things are as they are; still less are they a sort of high command which in some way forces nature to obey it. So the ideas of 'breaking the laws of nature', and of being 'inexplicable by natural laws', simply fall to the ground – they reveal misunderstanding of what 'natural laws' are.

'Something which excites wonder' is a very subjective definition, since what amazes one observer may leave another unmoved. The *Penguin English Dictionary* definition implies that inability to explain something is a reason for saying that God did it. From this it is a short step to saying that events we can explain are not God's work – and then we cut God down to size as we improve our explanations.

'Inexplicable events that happen as a result of prayer'[1] is another attempt at definition – but this is also difficult. For the believer, the explanation is simple – 'God did it'.

---

[1] *Church of England Newspaper*, Oct. 3, 1986, p. 5 in an article on a video, *The Healing Ministry*, produced by the Churches' Council for Health and Healing, St Marylebone Church, Marylebone Road, London NW1 5LT.

For the unbeliever, any explanation, however improbable, is better than the suggestion that God was at work.

So I believe we will do well to avoid the word 'miracle' (and similarly 'supernatural') for the following reasons: (i) it is ambiguous as used in current English; (ii) it appears incapable of scientific definition; (iii) it does not exactly correspond with biblical expressions.

Biblical words for 'signs and wonders'

The idea of 'signs and wonders' is expressed in the Old Testament by various Hebrew (and Aramaic) words, especially *ot* (plural *otot*) 'sign', and *mofet* (plural *moftim*) 'wonder'.[2] *Ot* is used both of quite ordinary things which have some special purpose or meaning (*e.g.* the commandments in the phylacteries of Dt. 6:8), and of remarkable things that point to something beyond themselves (*e.g.* signs done by Moses, Ex. 4:9). *Mofet* is often used together with *ot*, and usually refers to a remarkable thing (*e.g.* the wonders done by Moses and Aaron, Ex. 11:10; and the wonders in the heavens, Joel 2:30).

In the Septuagint, *ot* is commonly translated by Greek *sēmeion* (plural *sēmeia*), and *mofet* by Greek *teras* (plural *terata*). These two Greek words are found in the New Testament also. *Sēmeion* is used, for example, of the 'sign of circumcision' (Rom. 4:11), but more frequently of things remarkable in themselves, such as the 'great signs from heaven' (Lk. 21:11). *Teras* is used (in the New Testament only in the plural, and always together with *sēmeion*) of wonders done by Jesus and his followers, and of wonders to be done by false Messiahs (*e.g.* Mt. 24:24; Jn. 4:48; Acts 6:8).

This brief account is a considerable simplification, as it omits a number of other Hebrew and Greek words for wonderful things, and it does not describe areas of overlap, or points of distinctiveness, in their meanings. However,

[2] For further words, and fuller details, see the standard Bible dictionaries, *e.g. The Illustrated Bible Dictionary* (IVP, 1980), under 'miracles' and 'sign'.

I believe that: (i) it represents the essence of the biblical vocabulary correctly; (ii) it shows that from the biblical point of view it is reasonable to speak in English of 'signs and wonders' (rather than of 'miracles'); (iii) examination of the usage of these words in the Bible shows that they are most frequently used there to refer to wonderful things that are attributed to God's activity, and point beyond themselves to illustrate the character and activity of God.

Problems in traditional ideas of the miraculous

From my childhood I remember an occasion of drought when prayer was offered for rain first by the local Anglican church, and later by the Baptists. It was the Baptists' prayers which were most immediately followed by a downpour. No doubt this was a blow to other denominations, and to those who were praying for dry holiday weather!

It is easy to use stories of this kind to raise queries about 'God's intervention', to suggest that God acts capriciously and shows favouritism, and to trivialize prayer. More seriously, writers such as John Macquarrie have suggested that traditional ideas of miracle are 'irreconcilable with our modern understanding of both science and history', and also 'objectionable theologically'.[3] The theological objection he raises is that it is mistaken to expect God to prove himself in some extraordinary way. Early Christian writers, he says, put little weight on miracles, Jesus condemned the wonder-seeking attitude, and 'what is distinctive about miracle is God's presence and self-manifestation in the event'.[4]

Macquarrie is, I believe, right to hold that God's presence and activity in any particular event are only seen by faith. But he goes too far in minimizing publicly recognizable remarkable events in, for example, the exodus from Egypt, the ministry of Jesus, and the lives of the saints. Historians, it is true, have frequently dismissed narratives

[3] *Principles of Christian Theology*, rev. ed. (London, 1977), pp. 248–249.

[4] *Op. cit.*, p. 250.

of wonder-working saints on the grounds that they were the product of unscientific attitudes, and that comparable events do not happen today. The second of these assumptions, however, must be queried – comparable events do occur today, and I have personally witnessed a few.

Medically more satisfying than my personal observations is a study, now frequently referred to, by Dr Rex Gardner, 'Miracles of Healing in Anglo-Celtic Northumbria as Recorded by the Venerable Bede and his Contemporaries'.[5] He shows that a number of 'miracles' recorded by Bede in graphic but non-scientific language have modern parallels for which full medical documentation is available.

If it is allowed that 'miracles' (in the sense of remarkable events inexplicable in human terms) do happen today, are at least some of them examples of 'God's intervention'? I was present at a Christian meeting when the leader said he believed God would heal some deaf people; he invited the deaf people present to stand. A man near me stood, and I was actually looking into his face as an expression of amazement came over him and he said, 'I've been healed'. It is not difficult to raise objections – if the man had been very deaf, he would not have heard what was said, he may have been emotionally 'prepared' for healing, and if some deaf are healed, why not all? Having carefully observed the circumstances, however, I am satisfied that
(i) this was an instance of God's sovereign work in healing, at a time of prayer;
(ii) it was an example of exercise of spiritual gifts of the recognition of God's will[6] (and not a case of 'attempted manipulation' either of God or of the person healed);
(iii) it was an instance of 'God's intervention' in the sense of being a specific, observable, remarkable event associ-

---

[5] *British Medical Journal*, vol. 287, 24–31 December 1983, pp. 1927–1933. The article is summarized in D. Bridge, *Signs and Wonders Today* (IVP, 1985), pp. 163–165, and referred to, *e.g.* in J. Wimber with K. Springer, *Power Healing* (London, 1986), p. 296. Now see also R. Gardner, *Healing Miracles* (London, 1986).

[6] For a social anthropologist's study of such gifts see J. Wimber, *Power Healing*, pp. 252–273.

ated with prayer to God;

(iv) it was an example of 'seeking and receiving' in the sense that if the person healed had not gone to that meeting, or had failed to respond to the invitation, he would not have received healing at that time and in that way.

Theology, science and philosophy must, I believe, come to terms with the fact that such events are not uncommon today, and that for substantial numbers of them reliable documentation is available.

Medicine and prayer

It is not difficult to set up some sort of opposition between 'medical healing' and 'healing by divine intervention'.[7] Some people face it as a practical dilemma – should they go first to their doctor or to their church? Christian ministers may be faced by enthusiasts who 'won't go to doctors' or 'throw away their drugs' – or, on the other hand, by those who regard prayer for healing as virtually the last rites, a desperate attempt when all else fails. Sometimes it is implied that medicine is more 'appropriate' to some conditions, and prayer to others; this may prove to be only a short step from seeing prayer merely as a last resort for chronic psychiatric conditions. Also, some suggest that where medical services are well developed, God rarely heals without the use of such agencies, while he may do so more frequently when medical services are unavailable.

Such contrasts between medicine and prayer are, I believe, false. Medicine rightly practised is one of God's good gifts, and Christians are told to pray for the sick. I know a number of Christian doctors who quite specifically pray for healing with their patients. When I am praying for or with someone who is having medical treatment, I normally include prayer for the medical personnel involved; if it is appropriate, and the person permits, I communicate to the doctor the fact that we are praying. Close liaison between doctors and ministers is on

[7] For further discussion see J. Wimber, *Power Healing*, pp. 26–28.

occasions hampered by questions of confidentiality, but in general I have not sensed that prayer for healing is resented as interference. I hope that it will become commoner for doctors to take the initiative in suggesting to Christian patients that Christian friends might be involved in prayer for healing. I am told that awareness that the 'whole person' has to be treated is currently increasing among newly-qualified doctors; however, it remains true that links need to be strengthened between hospital chaplains, medical staff, and other Christian ministers, between hospitals, doctors, and Christian congregations, and between social services and church 'care networks'.

To the straight question, 'I'm ill; where should I go for help?' my normal answer is, 'Request prayer after the pattern of James 5, and go to your doctor' (in that, or the reverse, order). I only give a different answer if I believe that God is clearly revealing, through gifts of insight and knowledge, that he wills some other course of action, and I look for specific confirmation in such cases. In practice, the Christian minister or counsellor is more commonly facing people who have asked for prayer, rather than people who are asking whether or not they should seek medical help – so the question of advising about a choice only seldom arises.

A more difficult problem arises with conditions where evil spiritual influence is suspected. In the gospels there are many examples of people who needed to be freed from unclean spirits, and in some cases the presenting symptoms were conditions such as the inability to speak or hear (*e.g.* Lk. 11:14). If we accept the gospel accounts, we may suppose that *any* presenting symptom *may* (and *may not*) be of evil spiritual causation. Where such causation is in fact operative, medical treatment is inappropriate, and 'exorcism' or 'deliverance' is necessary; equally, where it is not operative, 'exorcism' or 'deliverance' is inappropriate.[8] Spiritual discernment, the gift of distinguishing spirits, is needed for diagnosis. The difficulties and uncertainties in

[8] For a summary of current debates on this subject see G. Twelftree, *Christ Triumphant: Exorcism then and now* (London, 1985), pp. 11–19.

this area highlight the need for careful consultation between doctors and ministers.

Authority

The New Testament gives examples of various models of ministering healing.[9] Frequently a word of command is used – 'Be clean' (Mk. 1:41); 'In the name of Jesus Christ of Nazareth, walk' (Acts 3:6). Sometimes a condition is 'rebuked' (Lk. 4:39). On occasions no words are used (Mk. 5:27–29). Physical contact is involved in some cases, and not in others.

For the disciple of Jesus who is attempting to learn and follow these models, an obvious dilemma concerns knowing when 'authoritative' language should be used. The source of power and authority is God – but when is the disciple to say, 'In the name of Jesus, be healed', and when 'Lord, I pray that you will heal'?

In answering this question, the fundamental consideration is that we, like Jesus, should be doing the Father's will. The Father's will is revealed through the Scriptures, and specific guidance, in accord with scriptural teaching, may be given through gifts of knowledge, wisdom and insight. If, therefore, I believe that in a specific instance it is God's will to heal, I use the language of authority, while recognizing God as the authorizer and source of power. If I am less certain, I use the language of praying for healing. And if I believe that the matter requested is not at all in accordance with God's will, I decline to pray.

It seems to me curious that while most Christians agree that Jesus' disciples are given authority to pronounce God's forgiveness of sins,[10] rather fewer agree that they have authority to chase away evil spirits, and probably fewer still recognize that they have authority to heal people

[9] For a summary see *e.g.* J. Wimber, *Power Healing*, pp. 249–250.

[10] See *e.g. The Book of Common Prayer* of the Church of England, in morning and evening prayer: 'Almighty God ... who ... hath given power and commandment to his Ministers, to declare and pronounce to his people, being penitent, the Absolution and Remission of their sins'.

in Jesus' name.[11]

'Signs and wonders' in other names

It is clear from Scripture that real signs and wonders can be done by 'false Christs' and 'prophets of falsehood' (*e.g.* Mt. 7:22; Mk. 13:22; Acts 8:9; Rev. 13:13), and also that the name of Jesus can be invoked improperly but effectually by non-believers (Acts 19:13–16). Subsequent history confirms that healings and other wonders can be brought about in the names of other gods and of demonic powers.

Recently I heard of a Christian lady who was advised by her optician that she probably needed a cataract operation. She replied that she would ask her church to pray for guidance and possible healing, and was told by the optician that he knew that a similar case had been healed through prayer at the local spiritualist meeting place. There seem to be four common reactions to such a story: (i) to claim that spiritualists are 'really Christians'; (ii) to claim that all, or most, religions are equally viable ways of meeting with God; (iii) to query the reality of the alleged healing; (iv) to recognize that other principalities and powers currently have real, though limited, power, while being ultimately subject to God. I believe that in general (iv) is the correct reaction, while in specific instances (iii) may also be correct.

Christians, I suggest, need to note certain warnings here: firstly, we are not to attempt to counter magic with magic. The Christian 'doer of signs and wonders' is acting with God's power in obedience to him; he must not be, or appear to be, some sort of magician or manipulator of God. Secondly, if we take seriously the scriptural statements about false prophets, sorcerers and the like, we cannot simply say, 'So-and-so was healed, so it must have been the Holy Spirit'. Where healing has taken place in a context of Christian prayer, it is clearly attributable to the

---

[11] See Matthew 9:1–8 and J. Wimber's comments in *Power Healing*, pp. 65–66.

activity of the Holy Spirit. Where 'natural healing' has been sought, or healing through names other than Jesus is involved, the healing is still presumably *ultimately* attributable to God's activity. I believe, however, that it is wrong to seek healing through other names, as it opens up the possibility that individuals who receive such healing may enter into bondage to other powers. 'Natural healing' (so-called) is of many differing varieties, and Christians who might seek it should ask on what philosophy or conceptual framework it is based. My own experience of such healing groups suggests that at least some operate on a distinctly non-Christian philosophical base; where that is the case, their work is open to the objection already referred to in connection with healing in names other than that of Jesus.

It is wherever the real article is to be found that copies and imitations, distortions and abuses are most likely to abound. Christians do not normally stop listening to sermons just because they hear a few bad ones. Similarly they should not be disconcerted and back away from signs and wonders, and the exercise of spiritual gifts, just because of some reason such as contemporary interest in the paranormal. The corrective to abuse is right use, and not disuse.

John 14:12

'He that believeth on me, the works that I do shall he do also, and greater than these shall he do, because I go to the Father.' This is William Temple's translation of John 14:12, and in his commentary on it[12] he interprets 'greater' to refer to the world-wide spread of the works of Christ wrought through his disciples. Michael Green similarly takes 'greater' geographically – 'After his return to the Father . . . the disciples would achieve far more than he had himself done, because the Spirit of Jesus, now no longer limited by a human body, but resident within their

---

[12] W. Temple, *Reading in St. John's Gospel* (London, 1961), pp. 226–227.

personalities, would empower them to be Christ's witnesses in word and deed throughout the whole known world'.[13]

In the writings of some commentators one can sense embarrassment about this verse. If the disciples of Jesus are meant to do the works that Jesus did, and that he instructed his first disciples to do, how is it that there are large areas of his ministry which are unparallelled in the commentator's experience? Some pass over the verse in relative silence. Others point out 'works' which have obvious contemporary parallels – 'the gathering of many converts',[14] 'the far-reaching spiritual effects which their [the apostles'] preaching was to bring about'.[15] While such parallels are true and important, they do not cover the full range of Jesus' works. R. E. Brown[16] seems to me more comprehensive – he says, 'Belief in Jesus will bring to the Christian power from God to perform the same works that Jesus "performs", and he mentions among these works "judgment", "bringing life", and "the power to perform marvellous works".'

I believe that John 14:12 means that Jesus commissioned his followers to continue the things which he did during his earthly ministry, which he instructed his first disciples to do, and of which we read in the Book of Acts. 'Greater', I believe, refers to the expectation that the disciples' activity will be on a wider scale (and perhaps of greater variety) than Jesus' personal earthly ministry.

Areas of probable agreement

In debate about healing and 'miracle' I have become increasingly aware of the danger of attacking stereotypes

[13] M. Green, *I Believe in the Holy Spirit*, rev. ed. (London, 1985), p. 221.

[14] C. K. Barrett, *The Gospel According to St. John* (London, 2nd ed., 1978), p. 460.

[15] J. H. Bernard, *A critical and exegetical commentary on the Gospel according to St. John* vol. II (ICC, Edinburgh, 1928), p. 543.

[16] *The Gospel according to John, xiii-xxi* (Anchor Bible. London, 1971), p. 633.

– of criticizing positions that no-one actually holds. The following is a short list of points on which I think most biblically-minded Christians would largely agree. It addresses the actual points made in a real controversy, and is based on a list intended to reassure various parties that their worst fears about the others were unjustified!

(i) The absolute sovereignty of God – he cannot be manipulated.

(ii) Jesus Christ as victor, saviour, healer.

(iii) The gospel as a message of salvation and wholeness extending to all parts of life.

(iv) The primacy of biblical teaching over experience.

(v) The guidance and work of the Holy Spirit.

(vi) The giving of spiritual gifts and the need to test them.

(vii) The fact that spiritual gifts are given for the building up of the church, and must be exercised within appropriate ecclesiastical authority.

(viii) The fact that, while we seek the Holy Spirit's guidance throughout our lives, our actual perception of that guidance, and our exercise of spiritual gifts, will be imperfect – that is, we will make mistakes, although we must attempt to avoid them.

(ix) The fact that divine action may be counterfeited by forces of evil, and that the goodness or rightness of a course of action cannot be judged narrowly on its immediate results alone.

How I am being changed

'If you don't think Roger's changed, you ought to have known him before' (remark overheard in corridor).

This autobiographical section is intended to show how my practice and expectancy have changed, and what positions I am reacting for and against. My father was a Baptist minister, and I was converted at the age of eight. As a student, I was much helped spiritually by the Cambridge Inter-Collegiate Christian Union, and by the ministry of the Rev. Dr John Stott at All Soul's Church, Langham Place, London. I became a member of the Anglican Church, and went to Ethiopia to work as a missionary teacher with the Churches' Ministry among the Jews, in cooperation with the Ethiopian Orthodox Church.

My wife and I both individually experienced increasing spiritual dryness, but didn't effectively communicate our feelings to one another, or know what to do about the problem. After fifteen years in Ethiopia and a shorter period in Israel, we returned to England, where I have been working part-time as assistant in an Anglican parish, and part-time as a theological college tutor. I perceived myself as in no way 'anti-charismatic' – yet when I told my wife that I had been asked to teach some sessions on the Holy Spirit, she replied, 'It's not quite your sort of thing, is it?'

The beginning of change for me was when one of my students spoke in tongues during a time of informal worship, and I realized that I believed I had been given the interpretation. (Prior to that I had rarely even heard tongues, and had never spoken in tongues or interpreted.) When I had spoken out this interpretation, another student prayed that the gift of interpretation might be confirmed, at which I felt a bit guilty, as I scarcely ever attended meetings where tongues might be heard. The gift was, in fact, to be confirmed a few months later, in circumstances rather more public than I might have wished. With hindsight I realize that these events fulfilled a prophetic word given through a friend a considerable time previously – and I had felt guilty about that also, as I had had no expectation of its fulfilment.

After this initial experience of interpretation, and for me partly as a result of it, my wife and I began to go to teaching seminars on prayer for healing given by Bishop David Pytches at St Andrew's Church, Chorleywood.[17] I found that the teaching was, with minor exceptions, what I believed in theory, but that my level of expectancy of answers to prayer, or of the exercise of spiritual gifts, had been very low. After I had got over the shock of seeing things actually happening as a result of prayer, I came to

[17] The content of the teaching has since been published in D. Pytches, *Come, Holy Spirit* (London, 1985).

value the practical experience that the seminars offered.

A little later I asked for prayer to receive the gift of tongues. I had over many years occasionally prayed for this gift, although I had always objected (and still do) to any implication that speaking in tongues is the principal sign of being filled with the Holy Spirit. I believed that I had been given spiritual gifts of teaching and administration, and I was not sure that God wanted to give me others – or perhaps I was too proud to ask for them, or fearful of disruption in a lukewarm spiritual life! Anyway, I did receive the gift of tongues, and questioned a number of Christian friends about the gift and its use. I found most of them more concerned with evangelism and prayer for healing generally than with the gift of tongues in isolation – and I began to realize in practice what was meant by those who said that the gift of tongues is commonly (not always) a gateway to the exercise of other spiritual gifts.

About this time some friends were praying for my wife for inner healing, and this had striking results, very evident to me in our marriage relationship. This led to an increased involvement for both of us in prayer for healing, especially 'prayer counselling' and 'inner healing', but also physical healing and deliverance. I learned that it is as God deals with us ourselves that we can also be his ministers to others. I became more relaxed about prayer – I expected to see some results, and I became less surprised if these results were sudden and dramatic, and less disappointed if answers to prayer appeared delayed. I also observed in myself and our friends some of the practical aspects of the work of the Holy Spirit in physical manifestations, and gifts of knowledge and discernment – and I wished that I had been taught about these sooner.

Subsequently, we have experienced a time of great pain, which has taught us about healing from resentment, about early steps in meditative listening prayer,[18] and about

---

[18] On this we found J. Huggett, *Listening to God* (London, 1986) and Brother Ramon, *A Hidden Fire* (Basingstoke, 1985) very helpful.

being broken and remoulded for God's service.[19] We are still too close to this to comment on it now, but we pray that God will keep us open to further change and will continue to change us.

How what I do has changed

Throughout my Christian life I have occasionally seen examples of remarkable answers to prayer, spiritual inspiration and guidance, prophetic words and 'words of knowledge'. However, until recently I had little expectation of seeing rapid healing or other observable signs of the Holy Spirit's work, at an actual time of prayer. I had felt that the witness of the New Testament and church history, to the effect that 'signs and wonders' continued in the early church, and at least intermittently throughout church history,[20] called for explanation. I had felt slightly embarrassed when teaching about spiritual gifts, and I had realized that I did not often meet with others for prayer and spiritual counsel.

It is with a great sense of relief that I now look back over the changes described in the section above, though they have not been easy. I am going to list some of the main results of the changes, as I currently perceive them.

Firstly, the time I spend in private prayer, prayer with my wife, prayer with other individuals, and corporate prayer has increased, simply from a desire to meet more with God. Enthusiasm for Bible study and worship has similarly increased, and I know a new desire *actually to worship* (rather than talking about worship or encouraging others to worship – why does everyone stay standing as they sing the *Venite*, 'O come, let us worship, and fall down: and kneel before the Lord our Maker'?).

Secondly, I expect to pray with people with greater immediacy. Formerly, if a friend said, 'Please pray for my aunt who is ill', I would go home and pray for the aunt

---

[19] On this I found Watchman Nee, *Release of the Spirit* (Chichester, 1965) very helpful.

[20] For a collection of testimonies from church history, see J. Wimber with K. Springer, *Power Evangelism* (London, 1985), pp. 151–174.

(or forget to do so). Now I will normally offer to pray immediately with the friend both for him/herself (the friend may be anxious, or be seeking guidance) and for the aunt, and I offer to go to lay hands on the aunt, or suggest that other Christian friends might be invited to do so.

Thirdly, I expect that at a time of prayer God may reveal himself through bringing to mind a passage of Scripture, through mental 'pictures' and words of knowledge, and through prophetic words and interpreted utterances in tongues. I now listen for these in a way that I did not before.

Fourthly, I expect that when God the Father is asked in prayer to minister through the power of his Holy Spirit, the Spirit of Jesus, to the needs of an individual or group, there may be physical manifestations of the Holy Spirit's work. These are very varied – a deep peace leading to a rapt expression on the face, sweating and shaking, heat and 'waves' passing through the body, inability to move for a time, collapsing on the floor semi-conscious, a sensing of a gentle breeze, a feeling of being 'touched' by God, and so on. I have myself experienced most of these, and this has been a help not only directly to myself, but also in interpreting these things to others.

Fifthly, I am much more ready to pray with laying on of hands, and/or with anointing with oil. These biblical models are increasingly in use in many churches – yet recently I found, for example, that many Anglican ordinands have never prayed for anyone with laying on of hands, and that more than half the students on a training course for ministry had never even *seen* an anointing with oil (of the type in the *Alternative Service Book*, Ministry to the Sick).

Sixthly, my readiness to be ministered to by others has increased. Formerly, I resisted confessing my sins to another (Jas. 5:16), and in general I expected to be giving out to others, rather than allowing them to be God's ministers to me.

No doubt there have been other changes, and there will be more – but these are currently the main ones as I perceive them, and I am grateful to God for them.

Reflections about a sore throat

At the beginning of a lecture I apologized for having a sore throat. Afterwards several students came forward and offered to pray with me. Within a few hours I was fully recovered, as a result, I believe, of their prayer.

When I told a colleague, he said, 'How do you know that other students were not praying for you silently, and so got you through the lecture?' I didn't, of course, know this, and I retracted any implication that the prayer of those who prayed *with* me verbally with laying on of hands was somehow superior to that of others who may have prayed *for* me silently, without physical contact, and without telling me. It remains true, however, that laying on of hands, and also anointing with oil, are biblical models of the ministering of healing (*e.g.* Mk. 8:23; 6:13; Jas. 5:14–16). In addition, faith is likely to be strengthened by a praying group actually looking for perceptible results. At the same time, it is possible for individuals to be deeply hurt when it is implied that their prayers are less effective because they do not conform to some special pattern or style.

The incident also raises the question, 'When is something too trivial to be prayed about?' If we are God's children, surely the answer is, 'When it is too trivial to concern *us*'. The sore throat did concern me, and I believe God answered prayer by healing it.

Colin Brown records[21] that he used to enquire about healing services, 'Did you see people healed . . . ?', and tended to get the reply, 'Well, people were helped a lot . . .'; but if he asked if people had seen something they would call a 'miracle' or 'supernatural healing', the only straightforward answers were negative. Two things need to be said: first, that I have seen 'supernatural healing', and have many friends who have witnessed it, beyond any reasonable doubt. Secondly, it is easy to underestimate the

[21] C. Brown, *That You May Believe* (Eerdmans, 1985), p. x.

importance of being 'helped'.[22] Many have been 'helped' out of a pit of chronic depression. I was 'helped' when my sore throat was healed, and when my back was prayed for three times and was healed in stages, fairly quickly, not dramatically, medically unprovably – but a great comfort to me and to the people who had been helping to carry my brief-case.

Encouragements and discouragements

My spiritual growth has proceeded in jerks. At various points there have been thresholds which needed to be surmounted. At the crucial stages it has been the encouragers who have helped me, rather than friends who urged caution, on-going debate, and a carefully balanced view.

The books that most encouraged and helped me in the area of healing are those by Francis MacNutt,[23] Agnes Sanford,[24] and John and Paula Sandford.[25] The people who have been most helpful are those who have taught and demonstrated biblical models for prayer, healing, and the exercise of spiritual gifts, in particular John Wimber and David and Mary Pytches.

However, I have also read books and moved in circles that I found discouraging, and a few notes on these may help the reader to see where I am coming from, and what I am reacting against. For example, Colin Brown's book *Miracles and the Critical Mind*[26] is a major examination and defence of the 'miraculous' in the ministry of Jesus, combatting those who for philosophical or theological reasons deny 'miracle'. It is a very valuable study. His

[22] See D. Bridge, *Signs and Wonders Today*, pp. 189–194, and, for a useful collection of very varied testimonies of healing, A. England (ed.), *We Believe in Healing* (Basingstoke, 1984).

[23] *Healing* (Notre Dame, 1974); *The Power to Heal* (Notre Dame, 1977).

[24] *The Healing Light*, rev. ed. (New York, 1972); *Healing Gifts of the Spirit* (first published 1949 and frequently reprinted).

[25] *The Transformation of the Inner Man* (South Plainfield, 1982); *Healing the Wounded Spirit* (South Plainfield, 1985).

[26] Eerdmans, 1984.

shorter book, *That You May Believe*,[27] however, I found discouraging to read. The emphasis is that 'the church has no specific ongoing mandate from Jesus to heal' (p. 192), although somewhat in passing (p. 204) Brown says, '[Healing and miracles as mentioned in 1 Corinthians 12:9–10, 28–30] have their place in the total ministry alongside other gifts and ministries'. If they have a place, what is that place? Experience suggests to me that many of those who reply 'a small place' are in practice denying them a place at all.

The editorial in *Anvil*, vol. 3 no. 2, 1986, pp. 97–99, is a further example of what I have found discouraging. It is a discussion of 'miracles, the demonic and biblical theology'. The writer makes four main points: (i) that miracles are for particular ends and are not the norm; (ii) that the biblical understanding of healing is much wider than that of physical healing; (iii) that the healings and exorcisms (of Scripture) are often much more restrained and sober than in . . . parallel . . . accounts; (iv) that by no means all illness in the New Testament is demonic.

I am in general in agreement on these points, though (i) is really a question of definition – would anything which is the 'norm' need to be called a 'miracle'? The tendency of the remarks, however, seems to me to be discouraging to the person who prays for 'miraculous' healing, or who is considering the need to perform an act of exorcism. The writer commends the advice of C. S. Lewis to 'pay as little attention to the demonic as is pastorally possible', and I agree – yet he does not go on to discuss what that amount of attention is that is the pastorally desirable minimum. It is a fact that demonology, exorcism, deliverance ministry and the like are not currently taught at all in the majority of Anglican theological colleges and courses. The average Anglican ordinand will not, it seems, know enough of such matters even to make proper referral to the relevant diocesan authorities. So it seems that 'as little as possible' in practice means 'nothing at all'.

Examples could easily be added. Some writers, wishing

---

[27] Eerdmans, 1985.

to encourage those engaged in patient but unspectacular ministry, effectively deny the 'miraculous'. Others, wishing to emphasize the supremacy of Scripture and the closure of the canon, effectively deny that God speaks today through prophetic utterance and gifts of knowledge and insight. Others, wishing to ensure that spiritual gifts are biblically tested, effectively raise a threshold so high that few beginners would dare to cross it. Others, wishing to avoid any divisiveness, seem to forget that the gospel itself does in fact bring division.

In all this there is a middle way of love, obedience and mutual acceptance, in which God is honoured, his varied activity is welcomed, and individual members of the body of Christ do not feel threatened by one another and by what God is doing to and through other members of the body. It is a difficult way to find, and probably always involves affirmation of our fellowship of sharing in Christ's sufferings (Phil. 3:10).

Conclusion

I conclude by saying that I believe that God acted through Jesus Christ to bring healing, and that he gives power and authority to his disciples today to heal; such healing may be termed 'miraculous' in the sense of being a wonderful sign of God's activity.

I apologize to any readers who find the tone of my contribution excessively personal. I am not a doctor, philosopher, or New Testament specialist, and I felt that personal reflections were all I had to contribute. I hope, however, that readers will not feel that I am elevating my own experience above Scripture, or looking askance at those whose experience is different.

I was reluctant to contribute to this book. I would rather have been spending the time 'doing the stuff', to borrow a phrase from John Wimber. However, I hope my contribution may be an encouragement to others to explore this area.

Response to Roger Cowley

Bill Lees

Roger Cowley has most helpfully underlined the wide areas where Christians agree. His list of nine points on page 96 will, I am sure, be accepted and welcomed. His fourth point is one I would want to underline heavily. Personal experience of God-given revival where 'signs' are prominent has confirmed to me that the devil's clever counterfeiting deceptions have not always been recognized. The problem is that genuinely revived Christians start fitting the Bible into their experiences of revival instead of subordinating their experiences to the total teaching of Scripture.

His eighth point, '... we will make mistakes ...', is also of great importance. Those of us who write and speak need not only to recognize our own fallibility but remind our hearers of the fact, remembering that the emphasis of the teacher or leader frequently becomes the excess of the less experienced Christian. I was concerned recently after attending a renewal meeting in Singapore with a very highly respected and godly Christian leader. I was suggesting that those teaching needed to be clearer as to what was actually being taught in relation to the work of the Spirit. My good friend just said, 'Bill, I have been crossing evangelical "t's" and dotting "i's" for decades and seen few of my contemporaries come to Christ. Now things are happening in their lives and that is what counts.'

True, 'the letter kills but the Spirit brings life'. Most of us have experienced periods in our lives of dry, dead orthodoxy but there are dangers in emphasizing experience more than the truths in Scripture which the Spirit longs to enlighten for us. Revival and signs and wonders must be seen in the total context of God's gracious interventions and not as a recently discovered missing key to effective Christian work or church growth.

Roger's approach, which could be summarized as 'I've experienced it, so others can', is an excellent way of encouraging growth in Christian experience, in prayer, personal evangelism and the like. I sometimes ask myself how else can we teach effectively? It was Paul's way (1 Thes. 1:6–8). When we follow that way we must also go along with Paul and see that we specifically teach 'the whole will of God' (Acts 20:27). Clearly Roger agrees. But we all know our hearers hear basically what they want to hear and in our existentially-orientated society, the emphasis on experience may be accepted without the general teaching and appropriate warnings.

Roger rightly comments on the need for and difficulty in distinguishing spirits and notes that there are medical situations where medical treatment is inappropriate. I agree the differential diagnosis can be very difficult. I also agree there are situations where exorcism and deliverance are necessary. Indeed I think it is appropriate to widen the issue, though it is not strictly in the realm of signs and wonders. Amongst animists (and increasingly in our own contemporary society) any turning to the Lord will have to involve a specific rejection of the devil and his works and a seeking of deliverance and cleansing through Jesus the Victor and Saviour. He came 'to destroy the devil's work' (1 Jn. 3:8) and to deliver people from all forms of involvement with the occult.

To turn more specifically to the limited areas where we disagree. On page 90 Roger comments on those who suggest healings are more frequent in areas where there are no (or only very limited) medical services. While I have no statistics to quote, I have an overwhelming impression from personal experience and from reports from other parts of the world, that the Lord is taking a direct hand in things more often in areas without the resources we take for granted. I do not see this as contrasting medicine and prayer but special provision not unlike 'manna'.

Then we should perhaps pursue the implications of John 14:12. I agree with Roger in quoting W. Temple and M. Green and underlining the wider geographical implications, but that expectation is basically of more (albeit much more) of the same. The verse in question speaks of 'greater' things not 'more'. I would see as an example of these 'greater things', the ministry through which God brought revival to a whole community in Malaysia so that the magistrates were put out of business for three years.

I think the discussion is complicated by the inclusion of 'prayer counselling' and inner healing. We can be most thankful that the area of inner healing has come to the fore in recent years. It has been going on, albeit to a lesser degree, for years before the present debate on signs and wonders. I can see why it is introduced to the present discussion, as it is an important part of healing and should be encouraged. However it is not really what most of us have in mind when speaking of miraculous healing or signs and wonders.

Lastly I am sure that Roger has a theology of suffering and dying. The fact however that it is not alluded to in his contribution highlights my concern that the signs and wonders discussion should be kept within a total biblical context of healing *and* suffering, living *and* dying, and not have inappropriate prominence. Let us rejoice in the grace that sustains us in a fallen world as well as the grace that delivers us from the consequences of the fall.

Hesitations about expectancy

Bill Lees

There is no doubt that God can and does perform miracles. The questions are why and to what extent he does them. They must fit into his overall plan for the church · God certainly heals by miracles. He is also deeply involved in healing that is not miraculous · There is no biblical or contemporary evidence that miracles and healings are the way to affirm God's presence. They probably have a special place in areas of new church growth, particularly amongst animists and other under-privileged areas · The grace of God is shown at least as clearly as he enables his people to cope with illness and suffering as in removing the sickness or suffering.

If God is God, how can there be doubt that he is able to perform miracles? For Christians committed to a belief in the authority of Scripture, the resurrection leaves the matter beyond dispute. He performed many other miracles in Bible times and he still does today. He also did many miraculous healings and is still able to do the same today. The question is, to what end does he perform miracles and to what extent will he work out the healing promised in Isaiah 53:4–5 in this life? Or must we wait for total healing and the end of all sickness at the second coming (Rev. 21:4)?

Any miracles, whether general or specifically of healing, must fit into God's overall plan for the church, part of which is that redeemed men and women should love him freely without coercion or bribes. This is something precious to God, otherwise he would surely not have given us free will. It is also something detested by Satan who insisted that Job only loved God for what he could get out of the relationship, and who presumably thinks the same about us.

Before we think about miracles, and more specifically about miraculous healings in our day, it seems appropriate to look at some of the occasions recorded in Scripture where God intervened. Why and when did he intervene? How does miraculous intervention fit in with the remarkable pattern of partnership in which God deliberately involves his people? Are there any indications as to what God expects the impact of miracles to be?

God, mankind and partnership

In the Lord's Prayer, we have striking affirmations of this partnership. Jesus teaches us to pray, 'Give us this day our daily bread'. This is not just a recognition of dependence. It is an affirmation that he intends to treat us as working partners. God provides the seed, the soil, the sun and the rain. We till, cultivate, harvest and process. Having worked hard, we are nevertheless thankful that it is he who has given us our daily bread.

He could so easily deliver manna to our doorsteps. He did this miraculously for forty years on a daily basis for all his people when there was a need to do so. Interestingly, however, he did not provide manna earlier for Jacob and his family when they were in great need, but directed them to Egypt. There they discovered that God had been working to provide for them over a number of years, well ahead of the crisis, in various and sometimes miraculous ways.

Later in the history of Israel we have magnificent demonstrations of his power and intervention: the sun stood still (Jos. 10), the story of Gideon (especially Jdg. 7:7, 9), the lifting of the siege of Samaria (2 Ki. 7:6–7) – to name but a few. We are left in no doubt that, when it comes to the conquest of Canaan, God could so easily have dealt single-handedly and miraculously with the situation, as he did in the case of Jericho. But he did not choose to do so, saying to Joshua, 'Now then, you and all these people, get ready to cross the Jordan river into the land I am about to give them – to the Israelites' (he is doing all the giving). Immediately he goes on to say that the land given will be 'every place where you set your foot, as I promised Moses'. God is giving them the land but Joshua and his people are to be involved in partnership with their all-powerful God.

For many years my understanding of God's view of mankind focused on his immeasurable love and his response through his Son on the cross to fallen, ungrateful, unresponsive, stupidly high-minded but insignificant rebels. In so concentrating on the fallenness of man, I missed out on another awesome aspect of God's attitude to us – his very high view of mankind.

He made us in his image. An image is exactly like the object reflected in a mirror while at the same time being totally different from it. In the same way we are utterly different from God and yet just like him. He is a person. Each of us is a person and in that sense, exactly like God. A simple working definition of a person could be the possession of an ability to handle knowledge, make individual decisions and respond with a full range of emotions. God made each one of us a person as he himself is a person. Then, having made us in his image, he treated us as responsible partners.

Partnership and healing

As Christians, we know we have nothing which is not a gift, whether it be the ability to concentrate, to reason, to coordinate movements or whatever (1 Cor. 4:7). By applying these gifts to medical science, researchers (who may or may not recognize the origin of their gifts) have been able to discover so much that is so helpful in dealing with disease and maintaining health. We in the medical profession have worked hard but medical advances are all as God-given as our daily bread.

None of us would see it as particularly Christian, especially spiritual or exercising faith appropriately, to say we will not sow seed, cultivate, harvest or bake bread but just trust the Lord to send manna or in some other way fill our stomachs. We are thankful for God's provision and to farmers and bakers. We gratefully eat the bread. The parallel with the Lord's provision through medical means is clear and we gratefully accept the provision. This is not, however, to rule out God's contemporary and direct intervention but rather first to give a proper and full place to what he has already done and provided so significantly in our day.

Miracles, the learning process and Pharaoh

We see God's respect for his creatures made in his image in his relationship with Pharaoh. Pharaoh was first *asked* to let God's people go. The evidence that it was not just Moses who was asking, but the one and only true God of Israel, was supplied in a way that most of us would classify as miraculous and very convincing. It is most illuminating to reflect on how many extraordinary and very public and openly predicted miraculous interventions had to occur before Pharaoh would respond and say 'yes' to God. These miracles must have been so obviously initiated by God – from Pharaoh's point of view, the God of Israel. As a series, all occurring at the time predicted, they could hardly have been seen as a number of chance events!

God was gracious and gave Pharaoh an opportunity to respond to this series before intervening in such a way that no 'explaining' or imitation miracle could 'dispose of' it as chance or whatever: the death of every firstborn – not just a member of most or even every family, but specifically the firstborn – in a single night, whilst the firstborn of Israelite families were spared. Pharaoh heeded this overwhelming evidence that God is God and that it is appropriate to listen to what he says and respond.

Pharaoh 'repented' as did all his people – evidenced by the gifts they showered on the Israelites. But the change of heart did not last long. We soon see Pharaoh going back on his miracle-induced repentance. There followed another miracle to save the Israelites from the pursuing army. Pharaoh rushed on in defiance and was overwhelmed. He had experienced the miracles but clearly he had not learnt to follow God's way. Miracles alone did not bring about lasting repentance.

Miracles, the learning process and Jesus

Dr Luke was enabled by the Spirit to see that miracles and teaching were interrelated parts of the ministry of Jesus. In Acts he opens the account by a reference to the gospel he had previously written about 'all that Jesus began to *do* and to *teach* until the day he was taken up to heaven'. The miracles are not an optional extra to the Spirit-enlightened physician. Healings had been prophesied as part of the ministry of the Messiah. The resulting crowds gave major opportunities for the Lord to teach either in relation to the healing itself or by more general parables or discourses.

In the story of the paralysed man, Luke records an example of teaching in the context of a miraculous healing. Jesus was teaching the religious leaders when the friends arrived. The entry was dramatic, the Lord's response even more startling: 'Friend, your sins are forgiven!'

The implication was crystal clear. Jesus was implying that he was God, and knowing what the religious leaders were thinking, he immediately reinforced the lesson by asking which was easier, to tell a paralytic to walk or that his sin was forgiven. The rest of the gospel leaves the impression that few, if any, of that privileged group really grasped that they were in the presence of God.

A couple of chapters later, we read of a centurion in whose heart God was working. He had a concern for the Jews and their faith and was responding very positively to what he had heard about Jesus. The Lord granted the centurion's request for the healing of his servant and then turned to the assembled Jews, pointing out that the Gentile had responded appropriately and fully to the healing of his servant.

The degree to which healings and miracles opened men's hearts clearly varied. John 6 opens with a crowd gathering as Jesus heals many. He then feeds 5,000 with five small loaves and two small fish. The crowd begins to assume he is the Messiah. Jesus crosses the Sea of Galilee and next day the crowds follow. He then teaches about not seeking 'food that spoils, but . . . food that endures for eternal life, which the Son of Man will give you' (Jn. 6:27). He goes on to teach around the theme of the bread of life. The crowds melt away and finally he says to the twelve, 'Do you want to leave me too?'

Significantly, in that chapter that starts with healings and a generous feeding miracle, he says, 'All that the Father gives me will come to me . . .' for 'my Father's will is that everyone who looks to the Son and believes in him shall have eternal life' (Jn. 6:37, 40). It's the Father who brings them, not the miracles. He also recalls that the prophets had written that 'they will all be taught by God' (v. 45).

Miracles and revelation

Peter and the other disciples saw many healings, deliverances and miracles and heard much teaching from the Lord himself. In Matthew 16 he is asked what conclusions he has come to about Jesus. He replies that Jesus is indeed 'the Christ, the Son of the living God' (v. 16). Jesus then asserts that 'this was not revealed to you by man' (presumably not by Peter's human capacity to put the evidence of the miracles *etc.* together to establish the case), 'but by my Father in heaven'. Miracles alone did not convince Peter. It had to be a special revelation.

There is no doubt that God is in the business of miracles. We can however be most thankful that it is certainly not his main means of revelation apart from the miracle of the incarnation:

> Our God contracted to a span,
> Incomprehensibly made man.   (Charles Wesley)

We have a major insight into Jesus' evaluation of the miracles, even the impact of the raising of the dead. He tells the story of the rich man and Lazarus (Lk. 16:19–31). The rich man asks that Lazarus should return to earth to warn his five brothers. The Lord puts into Abraham's mouth the words, 'They have Moses and the Prophets; let them listen to them.' The reply, 'No, father Abraham, if someone from the dead goes to them, they will repent', is met with the affirmation, 'If they do not listen to Moses and the Prophets, they will not be convinced even if someone rises from the dead.'

This is borne out by an Indian brother. He had a significant healing ministry but rated the gift of little value. 'They all come for healing and nothing more,' he commented. Little attention was given to the message of the God who graciously dealt with their diseases. It could have been 'just another healing', as Dr Angus Kinhear has documented cases of healings totally outside any Christian context.

In the UK the significance of healing is often written off by my medical colleagues with the comment, 'We agree the man had cancer, but we all know in some cases the disease stops and heals of its own accord.' All doctors know that that is true. For many it explains such healings most satisfactorily and eliminates the need of accepting divine intervention.

In Sarawak and Sabah (East Malaysia) the indigenous animist normally looks to the spirits for healing, especially in the interior where there is no medical service. Animists (spirit-fearing/worshipping people) and many other groups who live in the awful absence of any knowledge of God revealed in Scripture and in Christ, still know the reality of the spirit world and live lives full of the fear of offending the spirits. At times it suits the evil one to operate as an 'angel of light' and be helpful. Satan's healing is accepted as an activity of the spirit world in the affairs of men. Inevitably then, healings to them are not necessarily clear and definite evidence of the reality and nearness of God.

Tailor-made miracles

Miracles may not convince people regularly of the reality of God but that does not mean that God does not sometimes choose to work that way. Amongst the Tagals of Sabah, the Lord first used the witness of their former headhunting enemies, the Lun Bawang, to free them from the stronghold of Satan. The Lun Bawang had been miraculously changed out of all recognition from a group seen by the coastal Chinese as lower than animals to a community the local Chinese wanted to emulate. The Tagals too saw the change and wanted to follow the same way.

There was however another group of Tagals who lived further into the interior who had very little contact with the Lun Bawang. They were acutely aware of the authority and power of the spirits to whom they gave full and total obedience in all things. Twenty-eight years after I had joined with the first Tagal Christians in taking the gospel to this more distant group, we heard what God had done to demonstrate what every animist needs to know — that Christ is stronger than Satan.

At a convention in 1984, a lay leader told the 1,500 Tagal and Lun Bawang congregation about our first meeting. To him the message had been completely unacceptable. It had not been about the chronic alcoholism or habitual adultery which was sterilizing the community, but about the greatest sin of mankind — a failure to give God his proper place. The speaker went on to say that he had decided that it was necessary to kill me. He told of putting his hand on his jungle knife (everyone who lives in a primary rain forest carries one). To his amazement he could not draw it from its sheath. It was too heavy. He tried again but it was unbelievably heavy. He got the message very fast and announced to all that the spirit guarding me was stronger than any spirits they knew.

When we heard this it made sense of the experience we had in 1956 when we could not understand why everyone in all the villages in that valley wanted to follow Jesus. Politeness and hospitality were characteristics of the Tagals but equally there was an unwillingness to consider anything that would be contrary to the spirits. Yes, they knew of God. He created the sun, moon, hills and rivers, but why pay any attention to him? — he never harmed anyone. In this miracle God intervened (without our knowledge) to show that he was stronger than Satan, and that is what these Tagals needed to know.

Healing and young churches

Believers coming from an animistic background in areas where there is frequently neither a public nor private medical service, are going to look to the Lord and be encouraged by his provision of healing (provided we as missionaries have encouraged them to do so). Otherwise new Christians have no alternative but to look in the previous direction for help. God frequently meets their needs in miraculous ways. But he does not always do so.

Imagine the conflict in a village in another part of Borneo where there was a group of new believers. There was no older Christian or missionary to consult and two infants were seriously ill. One of the babies belonged to a new Christian family and one to a family who were still animists. The Christian family were learning to trust the Lord in all things. They knew God could heal. They prayed, believing. The infant died. The animist family went to the mediator with the spirits and the child lived.

Why, oh why did our caring God, who could so easily have intervened, allow this?

Part of the answer may be perceived in the history of the 'Jesus Family' that Dr Vaughan Rees was privileged to know in China prior to 1950.[1] It was an extraordinary group living as a community and sharing everything. If anyone was sick, the elders were called and many healings occurred.

Dr Rees told me of the day he was asked to join one of the elders in prayer for a critically ill child. The elder prayed and they had hardly stopped praying when the child died.

'Two years ago, it was unimaginable that we should pray and the child should die,' the elder had explained. 'But now we understand it is not healing we need but a deeper death. Healings are a good street to pass through,'

[1] Dr D. Vaughan Rees, *The 'Jesus Family' in Communist China* (Paternoster Press, 1972).

he had added, 'not a street to live in.' In the early days, the health of the body and the demonstration of God's power had apparently been the great issues. Later the concern was less for the physical and more for spiritual health.

The little family from Sarawak referred to earlier who lost their baby survived the trauma and progressed spiritually. In other situations, Christians have witnessed healings through the spirits and have been tempted to return to seek healing from them or through spirit media. When they have done so, some have been healed physically but have subsequently been overwhelmed by a deep spiritual darkness. In these situations, most specific repentance has been needed but, in the darkness, that is not easily understood.

Healing and 'rice' Christians

As we reflected on the death of the Christian infant, we considered that maybe God, in his wisdom and love, was not delivering these new believers from illness every time because the good (physical healing) could so easily become the enemy of the best (an ongoing relationship with the Lord). If being a Christian meant that, whenever a believer became ill, he had access to immediate release – the ultimate in medical insurance policies! – there would be an overwhelming flood of 'rice' Christians, *i.e.* those making a nominal profession as an acceptable concession on their behalf for the best deal available.

Fewer healings – harder guidance

Most of us have not grown up in or lived with churches emerging from animism. But many of us in the West pass through a parallel experience. Many older, mature and godly Christians will readily confess that guidance gets more difficult as we get to know the Lord better. For younger Christians there is often rather clear, possibly spectacular, guidance – guidance which almost comes through our senses – a voice, a vision, a Bible verse 'leaping out of the page'. Many of us have enjoyed (and sometimes, I can remember, gloried in) the experience. As the years have gone by, however, we have been weaned away from such guidance by 'sight' to walk more by faith without such sensory input.

We need hardly be surprised by this as we are told that 'without faith it is impossible to please God' (Heb. 11:6). We find the Lord is expecting us to reaffirm our commitment to him and world evangelism and then believe that he will enable us to choose the right path. For his part, he graciously promises to call us back onto the right path if we do happen to choose to 'turn to the right or to the left' (Is. 30:21). We must all, the former animist and those from the sophisticated West, learn to live by faith, even if sometimes that means trusting him through trials or in enduring sickness.

Illness and spiritual growth

S. D. Gordon, in his book *Quiet Talks on Prayer*,[2] tells of how he heard directly from D. L. Moody about the way in which the Lord had moved him into an extraordinary itinerant ministry on both sides of the Atlantic.

There was an older woman, a member of a well-populated but rather lifeless church in London, who was diagnosed as having an incurable ailment. When she knew she was to be house-bound she confessed to the Lord that she had done little in her active life and sought to know what her future ministry might be. God led her to start praying for her church. One day she read an article in an American paper that 'happened' to come into her hands. She was struck by a contribution from a largely unknown minister of a Chicago church and felt specifically constrained to pray that he would cross the Atlantic and preach in her church.

Meanwhile, during a period of rebuilding in Chicago, Moody had decided to visit other churches both in the USA and in the UK. He visited London and one Saturday

[2]Pickering and Inglis, 1986.

attended a prayer meeting. Having taken part in prayer, he was afterwards approached by a minister who asked him to preach the next day. The church to which he was invited was none other than the church to which the house-bound lady belonged. Moody preached to a very full congregation in the morning and had the hardest time of his life – not a glimmer of a response anywhere.

At lunchtime that day the chronically sick lady asked her sister, who had been at the service, what had happened. It was the question she asked her sister twice every Sunday and the discouraging answer was always the same. She asked it after every Thursday church prayer meeting too and heard the monotonously sad reply, 'The same old deacons prayed the same old prayers.' This Sunday however the sister reported that a stranger had preached – a Mr Moody from Chicago.

With great expectation the sick lady repeated her usual question. After hearing the answer, 'The same as usual', she prayed all afternoon, sure that this was God's time. That evening, Moody preached again and the initial response was as flat as before. But halfway through the sermon he could see some were understanding and by the end the congregation was so attentive that he decided to ask for a response from those who wanted to become Christians. Virtually the whole congregation stood! Concluding he was misunderstood, he asked them to sit down again while he explained his invitation more clearly. Again when invited the great majority stood. He asked the minister of the church how he understood the situation, but he too was equally surprised.

An after-meeting was quickly arranged and crowded out. Moody and the minister then decided to build in further delay and invited the enquirers back to a mid-week meeting. Still they came back. Moody was invited to take a full week of meetings. Four hundred believed and Moody began to move into his itinerant evangelism.

Moody reported this incident to underline that he believed that in the final analysis it would be seen that the unknown faithful servants who prayed were the key people in this great work of the Lord. I have repeated it because I believe it shows that the house-bound lady had a far greater ministry in her sickness than she had ever had (on her own confession) in her days of health. One does not, of course, have to become house-bound to become an intercessor. There are active people, and even activists, who pray – J. O. Fraser, Hyde, and many others. Many of us, however, are too easily diverted into other good things to do. I suspect the lady whose story Moody relates, rejoiced far more in the intimate privilege of partnership with her Saviour God in the house-bound years than in the days of full health and activity.

Disability and spiritual usefulness

Our eldest daughter was at first mildly and later totally disabled. We prayed for her together with a lady who had known many healings during her ministry. We believed we all prayed in faith for Ruth's healing and were actually astonished that she was not healed. Her disability increased rapidly from the age of ten and for the last two years of her life she was mentally and physically totally handicapped. She was able to see but could not look, to hear but not to listen. She was aware of people but could only just differentiate between us as parents and other caring adults. From the ages of six to nine she could speak a little and showed a clear love for Jesus. (The only time she said 'my' about anything was when she spoke of 'my Jesus'.)

She did however have a profound ministry to us, her parents, as well as to many others. Her life was a fourteen-year exposition to us of 1 Corinthians 4:7. Previously I had assumed that to be able to open a hand was a human right. To live with Ruth enabled me to understand that it was a gift from God. Indeed each and every capacity is a gift. A variety of folk who had contact with her were enriched in different ways. A prisoner in Parkhurst heard of her and his life too was touched. As far as we could understand, her life was a greater ministry than either of our other two daughters (both normal and active Christians) in their first fourteen years of life. We faced deep questions in this situation. Are we normally preoccupied with health and well-being rather than the glory of God and usefulness in his service? The salutary answer was a resoundingly clear 'yes'.

Paul's experience of praying three times about a problem from which he was looking for release is illuminating. There is no reason to suggest that Paul was lacking in faith and as time moved on he could see the wisdom of his Lord in leaving things as they were. Even such a godly man as Paul was helped and guarded by what he describes as 'a messenger of Satan, to torment me' (2 Cor. 12:7).

While we are not 'of the world', we do live in this fallen, disjointed and twisted environment. In some parts, the disease and suffering resulting at times directly from the selfishness and ambition of man reaches horrendous proportions. Clearly our God is not at a loss in finding ways to sustain his people. Their faith often shines brightly, burnished in the context of suffering. His glory is manifested in his keeping rather than through healing.

Some twelve months ago, I was introducing a godly Indian brother to a group in this country. I spoke of the poverty of his area as it seemed appropriate that the group of mainly European men and women should register that basically all of us in the West are affluent by comparison with our Indian brother's situation. In his response, he most graciously asked that we did not pray that he and his brethren should be released from their poverty. He had seen too much of what riches had done for us in the West. We were not offended but were aware of a timely warning from the Lord.

It is arguable that so much of the West's wealth is related to the fact that we are Christians.[3] We have been blessed[4] materially but many of us would confess that we

[3] See summary of the Weber-Tawney thesis in the appendix to *The Christian in Industrial Society* by Sir Fred Catherwood (IVP, 1980).

[4] Gordon MacDonald goes so far as to query whether we should call it 'blessing'. 'Surely,' he writes, 'something is not a blessing if it seduces us away from inward spiritual cultivation.' *Ordering your private world* (Highland Books, 1985).

look to the Lord more and express fuller dependence on him when things are not going well. At times when we have not known where our next meal was coming from and the larder was empty, our consciousness of dependence on the Lord has been much clearer than it so often is. In a straightforward easy situation, the temptation to depend on our own strength and resources (which of course are God-given) is one into which we often fall.

The more I reflect on the total situation, the more I see the significance of Romans 8:28–29. He *does* work all things for good for those who love him. He is not only caring, he is absolutely sovereign. His sovereignty covers all evil. It is reassuring to check through the Book of Revelation, especially chapters 6 and 7, and see how many times we are told that evil 'was given power' in certain directions but told not to touch this or that. God does not send any evil but he sets bounds and limits directly or indirectly on all evil. He knows the pressures will be great, but he has seen fit to allow the enemy some freedom until the final judgment. The enemy uses that freedom to seek by every means to undermine the relationship between God and his people. The end of Romans 8 summarizes Paul's confidence in the face of the problems (whatever their shape):

> I am convinced that neither death nor life, neither angels nor demons, neither the present nor the future, nor any powers, neither height nor depth, nor anything else in all creation, will be able to separate us from the love of God that is in Christ Jesus our Lord (Romans 8:38–39).

Revelation looks forward to the day when the enemy will be banished. There will then be no more suffering and we will enjoy our sickness-free new bodies.

Healing in God's will – the wider perspective

So far you, the reader, may well be coming to the conclusion that I am expressing a too negative attitude and underrating the Lord's capacity or willingness to heal.

Maybe it is because I have had the privilege of involvement with young, dynamic, growing churches, churches that were charismatic before there was a charismatic movement in the West. I have worshipped with churches that have had the privilege of revivals and seen congregations, and indeed whole communities, changed – areas where the magistrates have been put out of business for three years because of the effect of the revival on village after village.

Amongst these people, healing was not a problem area. There was great readiness to use the means the Lord provided with the same thankfulness with which they ate their daily rice. It was also assumed that you prayed for the Lord's healing at all times and especially when medicines were not available or were ineffective. God's direct intervention was sought and expected.

This led to the considerable embarrassment of a good friend of ours who was visiting from the UK and new to the area. He was not really accustomed to praying about illness. He had always been very fit and well himself and had always lived in areas where medicines and expertise were readily available. A young couple came to see him. He was clearly an older man and presumably an experienced Christian. Therefore they asked him to pray for their rather ill and fevered child. He was out of his depth and humbly told the Lord so. Clearly he should not cause the young couple to stumble or encourage disbelief. He did not want to suggest that God was less interested in illness than were the spirits. He prayed. The Lord responded and the fever disappeared. Both he and the young couple gave thanks to God and were strengthened in their faith.

There have also been situations (as in the story told earlier) where healings have not occurred. In these cases we have learnt so much from people's humble acceptance of God's will. There is deep grief, of course, but no recriminations about who lacked faith or blaming God for lack of love. There is rather an acceptance that it must be said of all that we have, 'the Lord gave, the Lord has taken away – may the name of the Lord be blessed' – the words of a man who knew more sickness, loss and suffering than any of us, yet who also rejoiced in eventual full healing and extraordinary blessings.

I am distinctly concerned about the spread of 'prosperity theology'. It is true that God blesses us in our work and in home and family life. He blessed Peter in his professional career beyond his wildest dreams (Jn. 21). It is not the story of the one that got away but of all the 153 large ones landed without any damage to or loss of tackle. But almost immediately Jesus asks the challenging question, 'Simon, son of John, do you truly love me more than these?' (more than God's prospering of his professional career). Peter affirmed that he did love the Lord more than the Lord's blessing and was commissioned to 'feed my lambs'.

God does so frequently bless us in giving us success and health, but what do our brothers and sisters in Siberia make of Western glorying in prosperity as if it is a normal part of being a Christian? What do our sick and starving brothers and sisters in Africa make of our assumption that to be well and well fed are part of being Christian? Our understanding of God's ways must encompass Siberia and suburbia, Africa and affluence simultaneously. Our understanding of healing, health, freedom from disease, must be global. It must encompass all God's people, including those in areas of endemic diseases and minimal, if any, medical services, as well as those in areas of excellent health and vast medical resources. I fear a preoccupation with health, the good life and long life could become a distraction. We are the people of God, witnesses to Christ, committed to world evangelism. We are called to care for all, particularly the lambs. And never in the history of the church have there been so many who are so short of teaching and Scriptures.

Dying

While we seek to align ourselves with the Lord's view of healing, we may do well to look at what the Bible says about dying. The New Testament is excited about that part of our salvation which is not yet revealed. 'We are children of God, and what we will be has not yet been made known' (1 Jn. 3:2). There is 'an inheritance that can never perish, spoil or fade – kept in heaven for you, who through faith are shielded by God's power until the coming of the salvation that is ready to be revealed in the last time' (1 Pet. 1:4–5). What the Spirit inspired John and Peter to write was clearly also part of Paul's expectation; to die or live – that was the difficult choice for him.

It is a difficult question for all of us, particularly as we think of those we leave behind for whom we might do more. But are we clear enough, in our collective thinking and teaching in our churches, about dying? The last enemy has been completely overcome. I think of a friend of mine who was ill with widespread cancer at the age of about seventy-five. His friends prayed for his healing while he and his lovely wife came to the point where they were ready for him to move on to the fullness of his salvation and meet the Lord he loved. After his death the good and close friends were so confused and disorganized by his death that they could not at first bear to come to the home and comfort the wife. She had to go and comfort them.

Our daughter Ruth was almost dead for two years. The Ruth we knew and loved was, in a very real sense, no longer with us. We had consequently two years of grieving time (*i.e.* adjusting to loss) before her body died. This gave us an opportunity, when she finally took her leave, to look at dying from her point of view rather than having to cope with overwhelming parental grief. I remember feeling so sorry for her because she had particularly laboured breathing, sometimes associated with dying. As I sat by her bed and held her hand, my thinking was switched to seeing her more as a marathon runner finishing the race, not in need of a chair to sit on but rather support right up to the tape. How lovely for her to reach that tape and to fall into the arms of her Jesus and to have a new body which worked properly and would give her freedom in his presence.

Healing in God's will in the UK

The creator produced a remarkable body with extensive self-repair capacity and a huge ability to deal with invasion by bacteria and the like. To this he has added a great range of knowledge and discovery of remedial agents. He has given governments which have organized health services.[5] We thank him and prayerfully accept his provision.

We pray expectantly and with thanksgiving about all things and that of course includes illness, as we take advantage of his provision within the medical services. As we do so we help to erode the division in our thinking (as those who have come out of materialism to Christ) between the secular and the spiritual spheres and see more clearly that our God is properly understood as God over all.

On rare occasions when I am sick and do not get better as might be expected, I ask myself if the Lord is seeking to say something to me or get me to focus on some sin in my life to which I've been turning a blind eye. Once when I put the question to myself, the answer was an emphatic 'yes'. I repented and was of course forgiven. I willingly undertook to apologize and make restoration of fellowship that was appropriate. The sickness resolved very rapidly! We should encourage each other to ask ourselves that sort of question, but I do not see it as a question one normally would press on others who are sick – only *some* sickness represents the Lord's chastening.

In other circumstances, when faced with an illness that remains unresolved in spite of medical help, we continue to pray, knowing that God is able to heal. But we need to focus on two prerequisites in prayer, namely faith and knowing the will of God.

We all know that it is by the exercise of faith that we please God (Heb. 11:6). Prayer in faith delights the Lord and alarms the enemy. His tactic is, I think, frequently to

---

[5] We should note that in this country and many others it was Christian initiatives that first cared for the sick. These were later taken over and extended.

press us to aim for a super-spiritual position and pray beyond our faith. I remember a medical colleague who had opened up a new practice, surprising 150 medical students at a conference where we were both speaking. When he said he normally prayed with his patients, the question was immediately posed, 'What about those who are disappointed with the answer?' My colleague humbly replied that he was not aware of any who had been disappointed. He had a 'golden rule' never to pray beyond his faith. If he did not have faith to pray for complete healing (and sometimes he did), he prayed for peace of mind or comfort or release from pain. He went on to say that characteristically the Lord's answer was over and above his asking.

Praying in faith is closely related to knowing the will of God. What was his will for my ninety-year-old mother? Her hip replacement operation had become a complicated two-stage affair. A skin graft to a bed sore had failed to take. She, in her own words, had 'had enough' of hospital treatment. I remember praying silently in the ward, 'Dear Lord, if you know she cannot grow further in her relationship with you, please enable her to die peacefully. If you see her as able to grow spiritually, please restore her.' She got better rather rapidly! During the next two years, as she lived a full and very active life, deep changes took place. At ninety-two she died at peace and peacefully in her sleep and her younger sister commented that she had never seen anyone change so much in two years, and certainly not a lady of ninety-two.

As we focus on the manifestation of his glory, it is immediately evident that his power may be demonstrated in healing or in the capacity he gives to an ordinary person or family to cope. We saw this in our own family with Ruth. Many will have read Max Sinclair's testimony[6] after his 'whiplash' fracture and partial recovery. Should we ask, 'Has God failed, firstly in allowing someone to drive into Max's car and secondly in failing to heal completely?'

[6] Max Sinclair with Carolyn Armitage, *Halfway to Heaven* (Hodder and Stoughton, 1982).

Max, after many months of reflection, sees the whole situation as a great blessing to himself and his family.[7] And we can add that to hear of, and see, God's enabling has been a real blessing to others also.

'Even greater things'

To what is Jesus referring in John 14:12 when he says we will do 'even greater things' than he has done? He healed the sick – those who had acute illness and those with chronic disease and deformities. He dealt majestically with demons. He controlled the storm. He organized the fish in groups or singly and indeed directed one to unusual activity so that it had the appropriate coinage in its mouth! Effortlessly he raised the dead when putrefaction was already well established. In this context he says that we (his disciples) will 'do even greater things than these' (presumably these miracles) through faith in him.

What can be greater than the range of miracles he did? Can he really mean more miracles? I do not think so. I do not think angels, spirits, demons, Satan himself, are particularly impressed with miracles of that sort. They themselves are very powerful and are able to do signs and wonders of a significant order. In Ephesians 3:10, however, we have a major clue as to what really amazes all spirits (angels as well as evil spirits). It is the 'manifold wisdom of God' made known 'through the church'.

Satan knows well enough what happened at the fall. He knows that the whole human race was spoilt and became self-interested and selfish rather than concerned for God and for fellow humans. We have already recalled his jibe at God that Job's commitment to God was only in self-interest. That members of this crooked, rebellious, self-seeking race could be reached by pure love (without coercion) and totally changed by the incarnation, Calvary and the resurrection, was quite mind-blowing for the spirits who know so well that fallen men and women are

---

[7] Max Sinclair with Carolyn Armitage, *Heaven on your doorstep* (Hodder and Stoughton, 1986).

really fallen. The glorious many-sided wisdom of God in wooing men and women to himself freely to confess their sin and repent (commit themselves to a completely different direction in life and accept his lordship) was and is the miracle which really impresses the spirit world which is itself accustomed to miracles.

The 3,000 who became Christians on the day of Pentecost were the first fulfilment, brought into the kingdom through a partnership between God and Peter. In our day the 'even greater things' are on a scale unimagined in New Testament times. Those who have responded to the marvellous wisdom of God in China in our lifetime, for example, possibly equal the total population of the Roman world in the first century. The transformation of the Lun Bawang mentioned earlier has had significantly more profound effects on their neighbours than any healings amongst them (these were not uncommon but soon forgotten). The transformation continues as a clear and incontrovertible testimony. Changed lives speak louder than other miracles.

Summary

God certainly heals by miracles. He is also deeply involved in healing that is not miraculous. I do not see that the Old and New Testaments, as well as contemporary evidence, present miracles and healings as *the* way to affirm God's presence, not even to Peter in his great confession.

Miracles and healings probably have a special place in areas of new church growth, particularly amongst animists and other under-privileged areas.

The grace of God is shown at least as clearly as he enables his people to cope with illness and suffering as in removing the sickness or suffering. We look forward to the revealing of our full salvation in his presence – totally healed and freed from all sin, sickness and suffering.

Response to Bill Lees

Roger Cowley

I want to affirm much of what Dr Lees has written above. I have not been able to identify specific points of substantial disagreement, but overall, I think there are three areas for further discussion:
(i) a difference of emphasis, probably partly linked to a difference of personal background;
(ii) some miscellaneous matters of detail;
(iii) the question of the authority and power that Christ gives his disciples.

Firstly, concerning our backgrounds, Dr Lees is a medical doctor; I am not. His missionary experience has been with young or revived charismatic churches; mine has been mainly in association with an ancient church that regarded 'Pentecostalism' as a threat. His experience of 'prayer for healing' has evidently matured over a long period; mine has changed recently in the ways I outline earlier.

As I look back over the last three or four years I ask myself why no-one had taught me previously about the Christian healing ministry, the use of spiritual gifts, prayer counselling,[1] and deliverance ministry. Perhaps I had been deaf to what had been said, but certainly I had not been shown *models* from which I could learn in practice. I am

---

[1] On which now see M. Pytches, *Set my People Free* (London, 1987).

therefore concerned that Christian ministers in training should gain practical experience in these areas. Such concern, however, is often countered with the points that Dr Lees has made about 'dangers of triumphalism', 'wrongly seeking signs', 'dependence on special revelations', 'rice Christians', 'over-emphasis on selected aspects of the Holy Spirit's work', 'prosperity theology', and so on. I hope that my position as outlined above is free from these objections – but critics have sometimes said that it 'tends' towards various specified errors. Then I feel stereotyped and get irritated! This may be the source of the unease that I feel about the tendency of Dr Lees's stories – what do they prove? I rejoice with him that a house-bound lady had a special ministry of prayer, and that an Indian pastor valued other gifts above the gift of healing, but I cannot from these examples draw general conclusions. I am sure Dr Lees is not suggesting that healing should never be sought for the house-bound, or that pastors should not value gifts of healing.

Overall, I find myself in agreement with the conclusions of Dr Rex Gardner in his book *Healing Miracles*, and I quote one of these:

> ... our experience today ... is that only a small percentage of those for whom physical healing is sought from God obtain it. But in absolute terms the number appears to be fairly rapidly increasing as more churches become open to this work of God; and percentage-wise more are being healed as the Holy Spirit is being permitted to develop ministries within local fellowships.[2]

Secondly, a few miscellaneous details:

(i) Dr Lees says, 'The question is rather to what extent he [God] will work out the healing promised in Isaiah now'. It is true that Isaiah 53:4–5 is cited in Matthew 8:17 in the context of healing (and elsewhere in the New Testament in other contexts), but I believe it is unhelpful

---

[2] R. Gardner, *Healing Miracles: A Doctor Investigates* (London, 1986), p. 206.

to link the question of God's healing work so narrowly to these specific verses.

(ii) He says, 'I fear a preoccupation with health, the good life and long life could become a distraction'. I agree – but so can any cause or ideal which is placed before Christ.

(iii) He refers John 14:12 to 'changed lives', and I agree that this is an important part of its meaning, but I still find it hard to believe that it does not *include* 'miraculous works' as well as changed lives.

(iv) In his summary, the sentence, '[God] is also deeply involved in healing that is not miraculous' seems to me to raise the problem of the definition of 'miracle' that I have addressed above. Also, I remain puzzled by the suggestion that 'miracles and healings probably have a special place in areas of new church growth'. No doubt they have 'special' (but various) places in all parts of the church. But I feel wary of assumptions that miracles 'ought to' or 'must' fit into some overall plan or theological schema – the danger is that we define the plan and then presume to decide what God ought to do.

Thirdly, there is little mention of authority and power in Dr Lees's contribution. I believe the New Testament teaches that Jesus commissioned and taught his disciples to preach the gospel, heal the sick, and cast out evil spirits, that he gave them authority and power to continue doing this after his own death, resurrection and ascension, and that this authority and power are available to his followers today. The power is God's; it can only be exercised in accordance with his will, and should not be used in any triumphalist, sensation-seeking, or boastful manner. It has been neglected by the church, and I want to encourage Christians to rediscover what the New Testament teaches about it.

Part 3
Healing in church life

David Huggett and Philip H. Hacking

A ministry to be encouraged

A ministry easily over-emphasized

A ministry to be encouraged

David Huggett

There are four levels of prayer for healing in church life, expressing corresponding levels of commitment: (1) Prayer for the healing work of medical and caring professions; (2) Healing prayer offered on the basis of James 5:13ff., without a clear understanding of what might happen; (3) Healing services with the laying on of hands, on the assumption of blessing for the person even if nothing dramatic happens; (4) A broad ministry of healing, signs and wonders where prayer is made for specific healing. Here faith – expectancy that God will act in significant ways – is a central strand of church life. The author is concerned with a church that is moving from level 3 to level 4 · Personal testimony · His own church, St Nicholas's, has its own statement of belief regarding healing ministry.

If we ask the question about our own church fellowships – 'Is God's healing apparent in my fellowship life?' – we must surely require a universal answer, 'Yes'. The question is not perceptive enough. We must discern between a developed ministry of healing and the universal agreement that in church we should pray and expect God's blessing on the medical and caring professions. This latter is an important prayer and one we find God answering. Church fellowships express their commitment to God's healing at different levels. Four different levels are as follows:

Level one: Prayer for the healing work of medical and caring professions.

Level two: Healing prayer offered on the basis of James 5:13–16, without a clear understanding of what might happen. The basic dynamic is longing on the part of the sick person, their call to the elders, and the elders responding to Scripture.

Level three: Healing services with laying on of hands and a wider availability of the ministry under level two. The assumption is now that such prayer will be a blessing to those receiving it even if very few receive anything dramatic by way of healing.

Level four: A broad ministry of healing, signs and wonders where prayer is made for specific healing. This includes 'the command of faith' type of prayer (*e.g.* Acts 3:6). Here faith – an expectancy that God will act in significant ways – is a central strand of the church life.

In this chapter we are concerned with the church which is moving from level three towards level four.

Changing levels of prayer – a personal reflection

For over thirty years of my Christian life I felt at home with level one, and vaguely uneasy about level two. I would not have entertained level three, and level four would have been for those that were over the top, unhinged even!

Ordination into the church ministry enabled biblical reflection and made me aware that level two had to be an option however little I understood its dynamics. I also saw that level three was widely honoured by God in other Anglican churches. Hopefully, I thought, it would not come to our church! I recognized that real pastoral work meant coming to grips with broken people in their unhealed state and lack of wholeness. Subconsciously I rejected any idea of physical healing and moved into the area of the emotions and the mind. Theological studies were augmented by attending an undergraduate students' course in psychiatry with a couple of extra terms on place-ment with a psychiatrist on a psychiatric ward. For my wife and I learning and experiencing counselling skills has been a continuing quest.

It took an encounter with the power of God through the renewal movement some thirteen years ago to remove me from an uneasy relationship with level two, through to level three, into an encounter with and involvement at level four. For me to be filled with the Holy Spirit also meant encountering in a new way the power of God, which immediately filled out my counselling ministries. Now when I began to reach the areas where healing was needed I was in touch with power that could change, release and make whole.

It was still to be several years before God placed me in a pastoral situation where I had to face the question, 'Did I believe God could heal physically in answer to my prayer?' I vividly remember the gentle but inescapable cornering of the Holy Spirit as God challenged me to pray for Barbara's physical healing as she lay stricken in the small room of the health centre. A few hours later she should have been sitting her final exam. After an agonizing hour of avoiding the challenge of prayer for healing I prayed directly for healing and left her. In the ensuing hours my faith wavered and slipped away. Several days later I learned that she had left the health centre some hours after our prayer, fully restored. Four weeks later she was awarded a first class honours degree. I do not know how she was healed. God did it. I had been caught up through prayer into God's work of power. I am no longer ashamed to consider level four as biblical and contemporary.

As a church here in Nottingham we see God at work on this level week by week and we are just beginning to learn something of our part in this work. In the light of our experience I shall reflect on the questions set out by John Goldingay to give this book a framework. Then I shall provide a little history of developments in our church and finally set out our approach, including our future aims as a church.

In what sense and on what basis can we take the signs and wonders performed by Jesus, and his disciples, and the church in Acts, as a guide to the healing ministry we should expect to see exercised in the church today?

To answer this we must look chiefly to the patterning of Jesus. We should expect to see his teaching reflected in

the patterning of Acts and teaching of the epistles. Jesus' ministry was marked by power and authority. He exercised this in at least five clear areas:
1. Speaking the word of forgiveness (*e.g.* Mk. 2:10).
2. Performing signs and wonders (*e.g.* Mt. 8:27).
3. Speaking the word of healing (*e.g.* Mt. 9:8).
4. Confrontation with Satan and evil spirits (Lk. 4:36).
5. Preaching an authoritative word (Lk. 4:32).

This power and authority is continuingly noticed and remarked upon by the people. Jesus makes it clear this power and authority is something which is given him by his Father. He derives it from his Father (Mt. 9:6,8; Jn. 5:26–27; 6:38; 10:18; 17:2). His word, even on the threshold of heaven at his ascension, is, 'All authority has been given to me'. The Father gives to his Son, the man Christ Jesus, the authority and power (compare Lk. 4:14–21).

In his lifetime, Jesus gives this authority and power to the twelve (and to the seventy). Thus he gives his power and authority to his embryonic church. At his ascension he bequeaths to his infant church this same anointing – power and authority. They are told to wait for the power which will equip and enable them for ministry (Lk. 24:49; Acts 1:8). The church is told that the Jesus of all authority will be personally with them (in them by the Holy Spirit) not just for the early years of the church but till the end of the age (Mt. 28:18–20). The texts of Luke and Matthew are parallel here. Luke says that it is the receiving of power that will send them out to be witnesses. Matthew in effect says that, because the Jesus of all authority is with them till the end of the age, therefore go and make disciples. . . .

We today stand under this great commission with its promise of blessing and its responsibilities. Power and authority are the inheritance of the church in measure as Jesus comes to us by the Spirit. It is not that the Jesus of some authority is with us and in us. It's the Jesus of all authority, and that includes areas two, three and four with which we are particularly concerned in this chapter.

The great commission (Mt. 28:18–20) leaves the church expecting to receive the passing-on of this authority and power. 'Teaching . . . to obey everything I have commanded you,' says Jesus. Proposition seven in the introduction (p. 17) says that there is no mention of healing here. Certainly there is no mention of it explicitly, but nor is there mention of the Lord's Supper, worship, and the like. About all these the Lord had commanded and taught his disciples. For example Jesus taught and commanded his disciples concerning healing. The church is to pass on, as required obedience in its disciples, these ministries of power and authority, just as it is to pass on the observance of the Lord's Supper, worship, and so on.

It will help here to quote proposition seven in full. 'Jesus' healing ministry, that of the disciples, and that exercised in Acts, demonstrate that Jesus' coming brings a new age. This ministry is reported as part of the gospel; it's not set forth as a model for our ministry. Where Jesus does commission the church after his resurrection, healing is unmentioned (except in the later ending to Mark). Healing in the gospels or Acts should, then, not be made a fundamental basis for our understanding of healing ministry today'.

There is in the proposition an artificial constraint. The implicit requirement is that ministry today may be patterned on that of Jesus and the gospels only if it receives explicit mention in the post-resurrection commission of Jesus. This is altogether too narrow a bottleneck. It is difficult in view of John Goldingay's experience mentioned in the introduction not to see this as an attempt to justify the theological position taken for other reasons.

Our justification for taking Jesus' ministry of healing, miracles, signs and wonders as a pattern would stand chiefly on the direct teaching of Jesus on this point. It will be backed up in the way he taught, trained and commanded his disciples on this point; how he directed them to pass this ministry on to others. It will be further undergirded by the record of Acts and the teaching of the epistles concerning these gifts and ministries in the church. Further support would be lent by the example and experience of the church down the ages and the contemporary witness of the church throughout the world.

Jesus settles our question for all Christians, for all time, by speaking directly to this question. 'I tell you the truth, anyone who has faith in me will do what I have been doing. He will do even greater things than these, because I am going to the Father' (Jn. 14:12).

We notice several things here: first the final phrase, which lifts the statement into the status of an ascension commission. Secondly, the introductory formula warns us that it is one of Jesus' crucial and very important sayings. Thirdly, its extent of application is not limited to the twelve, or the seventy, or the early church: Jesus says, 'anyone'. Fourthly, the immediate context indicates that Jesus has miracles, healings, signs and wonders in view. He does not say that anyone will teach what he has been teaching – the emphasis is on *acts*. Fifthly, the appropriateness of Jesus' works of power as a pattern for us is explicitly stated. Finally, time and change, far from leading to a lessening or ceasing of this work, will rather lead to greater things.

It is not necessary to argue that the early church in Acts is shown as walking in the Master's footsteps in this matter. The epistles clearly teach people to expect these gifts and ministries of healing and miracles. In some eight passages concerning gifts and ministries, at least twenty are spoken of. Many are only mentioned in one passage. Healing and miracles however are mentioned in three passages, and only three gifts and ministries receive greater mention than them in these passages.

Clearly the expectation and teaching of the early church was that it would continue to receive these ministries and gifts. The story unfolded by church history shows a continual thread but with shifting intensity and weakness which saddens the student. The same waxing and waning is also sadly present in the record of evangelism and missionary concern over the centuries. Graciously God has brought us back to an awareness of the centrality of evangelism and mission, so also now to the importance and centrality of healing and miracles. Those who minister and travel beyond Europe surely cannot fail to be confronted with the fact that God's ministry of signs and wonders is alive and well in his church today. Some returning missionaries tell me sadly what I know from personal experience: 'We cannot tell some church fellowships what we have seen because we know they will not believe us!'

What is the place of the ministry of healing in the life of the church? Does the ministry of healing belong in the context of regular public worship, or of some special services, or in the home, or of healing missions, or of healing centres, or what?

If we argue that this is a part of every-member ministry, then it is one which should be at home at street level. It belongs to the one-to-one (or better two-to-one) interface of home, marketplace and workplace. Worship and witness are also every-member ministries. All these personal ministries are intensified when the body of Christ meets together. Thus the ministry of healing, signs and wonders will have an expression in church gatherings, and as with other ministries will need careful ordering. From here on it will be helpful to speak increasingly about our own experience at St Nicholas, Nottingham.

In our understanding of evangelism we have moved from the showpiece Guest Service to much more of an emphasis of God's saving power being available at each service. In the same way healing services have been replaced with the ongoing continual expectation and offer of healing, signs and wonders. Specialist healing services promote personalities, elitist gatherings and divide fellowships. Big missions and showpiece guest services do the same and are similarly, we feel, not the best way forward. In our climate of disbelief and disarray, however, they may continue to be a necessary second-best in some situations.

Healing (and evangelism) are not helpfully seen as things which happen 'out there' where the spotlight is put on them – they are rather expressions of the united believing fellowship. They belong best and most happily within the context of worship and teaching about Jesus. Healing missions and rallies can so easily focus on healing and not on Jesus. In a sense, within the gathered fellowship the demonstration of God's power and healing should be no more remarkable or significant in its impact than the reading or preaching of God's Word. Equally powerful should be the sense of the presence of God as his people are caught up in praise and worship.

Where the Word, worship and healing power are held together, we believe that we have the most biblical and effective gathered expression of ministry. Where this balance is strangled or denied by the traditionalism of the fellowship or clergy decisions, the para-church meetings will thrive. These meetings can often be unbalanced in content and divisive in impact. In such situations we should argue for balance in such meetings rather than closing them down. We should also pray for a change of heart in pastors and traditional congregations.

In what way should we expect signs and wonders to witness to God's presence in power? How does such ministry relate to evangelism?

They are, as it were by definition, manifestations of God's presence and power. Whether they are seen as such depends upon the perception of the individual. This is how it was in Jesus' day, when the threatened, the spiritually blind, and opponents discounted, explained away, overlooked and trivialized them. So it is today, especially in the eyes of unbelievers, but also, sadly, as in Jesus' day, by some of those who fear God.

In our experience God meets people in St Nicholas with the reality of his presence almost equally through the power of worship, the ministry of signs and wonders and the proclamation of the truth. All these are evangelistic in as much as they raise the question, 'Sirs, what must I do to be saved?'

The prayer of the early church (Acts 4:29–30), the reflection of Paul (Rom. 15:18–19) and the witness of the experience of Acts would indicate the preaching of the Word was almost invariably accompanied by signs and wonders. The New Testament pattern seems to put them in partnership in evangelism. The two references mentioned say clearly that full proclamation of the gospel includes power signs. We believe that we should follow the New Testament pattern and to that extent be biblical in our evangelism.

When God acts in power, he is speaking. Space must be made to hear, listen and understand. Whenever God is at work his Word is being proclaimed; his name will be honoured, exalted and glorified; his people will learn, understand, see and worship. Those who didn't know him will encounter him. Encounter is the purpose and heart of evangelism.

Is it our business to attempt to discern when God might wish to do some signs by healing someone? If so, how do we do so?

Whenever anyone is prayed for in this way, especially if the request for prayer comes from the sick person, it is crucial to determine to the best of our ability if we are praying in line with God's will for them. Accordingly we must ask three questions:

1. Is this particular healing God's will for this person at this time?
2. Is this God's moment and place for this prayer?
3. Are we the right people to pray in God's name at this time?

Unless we have opened ourselves to these three questions we may act irresponsibly. Even if we open ourselves to them we may not hear the answer accurately. This is part of the inevitable need to grow in this ministry as in any other. It is the essential path of any person of faith. We walk by faith, not by sight.

Whether such a 'healing' is a sign in the narrow sense – that it speaks deeply to others – can only be in God's hands. We may not expect to know much about this aspect in advance. Thus Peter and John had the clear sense that they should pray for the cripple at the gate Beautiful, but they would have had little intimation of what would happen afterwards. Learning to discern the Lord's will, learning to listen to him, is a major part of the development of the individual in this ministry. To foster the ministry in our churches, our people need to be willing to learn. We need to be willing to teach them and to provide oversight and supervision in the learning process. Here we shall be helped by the example of Jesus. From this we shall learn much including the value of learning in pairs, apprenticing and modelling ministry.

Is it our business to attempt to distinguish between divine healing in answer to prayer, and spontaneous remission? If so, how do we do so?

All healing is God's gift, including 'spontaneous remission'. This question seems to be asking about the person healed after prayer: 'surely this sick person would still have been healed even if you had not prayed for them? The praying was just a coincidence!' If all healing is God's gift then we give thanks that we have received what we asked for however we received it. Ultimately God is behind all healing. Whatever means he uses we would want to give him thanks and praise. If he draws us by faith into praying in accordance with his will beforehand, then we shall also rejoice in being caught up into his inscrutable ways. Narrowly to assume that prayer is to alter what otherwise would have happened is fundamentally an erroneous concept of prayer. Jesus does not appear to have spent overmuch time checking the mechanism and analysing the results of his prayers for healing. In the last analysis the working of God is beyond our understanding but he calls us to pray for what we need and promises to hear our prayer. Jesus prayed and God answered; we pray and God answers.

What do you understand by the term 'Inner Healing', and what do you see as the role of this ministry in the church today? How does the ministry of physical healing relate to inner healing?

Many Christians are prevented from being really effective in their ministry by personality damage. An adult whose parents' marriage broke up in their formative years may find the fatherhood security of God difficult to relate to. A victim of incest may find it difficult to relate to the opposite sex. Traumas in the relationships between mother and baby in the first year of life may lead to damage in trust patterns in later life. Much of this pain is hidden in many of us. Many will never be inhibited by such experiences, but a few will become damaged people. Counselling can expose the forgotten pain and discover the root. Inner healing is the way in which God touches and heals such pain and damage and brings a greater wholeness to the individual. Through prayer for inner healing God may

- heal the hurt;
- bring to life a strand of personality or character which has been largely missing in a person's life;
- lance the abscess of stored-up poison (anger, resentment, and the like);
- break the power of the memory to hurt and to inhibit in the present;
- take away the 'sting' in the memory;
- cleanse the blood line;
- set the person free to live differently;
- open the person up to a new or deeper filling of the Holy Spirit.

As John Powell says, 'Our yesterdays lie heavily on our tomorrow'.

In our disjointed, harsh, competitive, unloving, materialistic and selfish Western society there are many hurts inflicted which are of a different order from those of a first-century Middle East culture. We therefore find this ministry far more widely used today than in the ministry of Jesus. We find a parallel in Jesus' ministry in, for example, the way he restores Peter after his three-fold denial at the crucifixion.

We are aware of the growing interest in holism with its biblical stress that body, mind and spirit are very closely interrelated. This reminds us that it is unwise to deal with the body, mind or spirit in isolation. Contemporary medical insight confirms that many physical symptoms have roots in disorders in the mind. We meet, for example, the person who has been hurt in childhood who has grown up with bitterness and resentment in almost every relationship and is now arthritic and approaching old age. Simply to send them for medical treatment may very well be inadequate. Disordered relationships will frequently lie behind the physical symptoms. If all we do is to call them to repent and live differently we are in danger of neglecting the root problems. These may well need inner healing followed by spiritual counselling for relationship problems. Such prayer ministry will quite often lead to considerable physical healings. It is essential in this sort of case to follow the spiritual counselling prayer with positive suggestions of how to build and maintain good relationships. Healing of any sort needs to be followed with instruction in living a new life.

What is the place for the rebuking of evil spirits in connection with the healing ministry?

Since we are to be like Jesus and share his ministry, dealing with the demonic will be part of our experience. Church history records the careful preparation in this area of new converts for baptism which was undertaken in this country before the so-called Christianization of Britain. In the Anglican liturgy for baptism the candidate is thus still required to renounce evil. Encounter with demonic activity is becoming more widespread in this country. It is also a common experience in many parts of the world to be confronted with fairly developed demonic activity. We need to be aware of demonization and how to deal with it.

Every Christian is involved individually to some degree in personal encounter with demonic forces. Some Christians are unaware of this encounter. Disguise has been a master tactic of the evil one since Genesis 3 (compare 2 Cor. 11:14). The teaching in the epistles on spiritual warfare equips the Christian to deal with this personal encounter (1 Pet. 5:8; Eph. 6:10ff.). There is a radical difference between meeting the onslaughts of Satan and his minions and dealing with the temptations which have their roots in our sinful nature. Thus we are told to flee from temptation but to stand our ground against the evil one (Jas. 4:7; *cf.* Eph. 6:11, 13–14). On the individual level if we fail to recognize the demonic we may react inappropriately.

There are dangers in teaching about the devil. We can give him too much prominence. We can attribute too much God-likeness to him (*e.g.* he is not omnipresent). We can excuse too much of our own failure by attributing it to demonic attack. The vast majority of our failure and sin is best understood in James's words: 'Each one is tempted when, by his own evil desire, he is dragged away and enticed' (Jas. 1:14). The reality and power of the demonic are clearly evident as Jesus ministers in power, and the link between this demonic activity and sickness is also clear. Too easily our Bible translators have led us to think that people are possessed by evil spirits, whereas the word used in the New Testament is better translated 'demonized'. This covers a wide range of conditions, only one of which, and an extreme one, would be actual possession. Most of the demonic activity we deal with falls far short of possession.

In our teaching we need to instruct Christians about the evil one and his nature so that they can recognize his activity and expose it. We need to teach a little about contemporary satanism. For example, many satanists are fasting and praying for the break-up of Christian marriages, especially those of Christians on the front lines. To teach this is to explain what we are doing and to allow Christians to bring the power of God against the enemy and defeat him. Not to teach about spiritual warfare is like sending off a transatlantic yacht with only a compass and no radar. It will probably get there but with some nasty experiences on the way.

Demonization presents us with people who are in bondage, oppressed, and occasionally possessed. Some of these will have presenting symptoms of physical sickness. Christians should be taught to deal with bondage and oppression, learn how to bind and rebuke the evil one, and understand the link between evil spirits and sickness.

James 5:13–16 seem to encourage us to assume that healing will always follow upon anointing, believing prayer, and confession. Where it does not, are we to infer there must have been an absence of faith on the part of

the elders, or that 'prayer of faith' is a special God-given assurance that God will heal in this case, or that the passage encourages us to expect that the kind of person it is talking about will always be 'saved' whether or not he or she is 'healed'? Or what?

The key to understanding this passage would appear to be in the two words in verse 15, 'in faith'. The scriptures give us many great promises which are available to those who ask or pray 'in faith' (*e.g.* Mt. 21:21f.). A large part of prayer is alignment, learning to see situations as God sees them, to feel the heart beat, to sense the will of God. The whole exercise of listening to God in prayer is to feel after an understanding of his way forward in each situation. When we know this we may pray in faith and God will answer. 'This is the assurance we have in approaching God: that if we ask anything according to his will, he hears us' (1 Jn. 5:14). Unless we believe in listening to God and know that we can hear him speak to us of his will for a particular situation, this verse will come back merely to mock us. We feel mocked because there is no confidence; we do not know if it is his will. In this case the only prayer I can pray is, 'Please heal if it is your will'. This prayer is unlike that of Jesus in the gospels and his followers in Acts, where there is ringing confidence that he will act.

The elders in James 5:13–16 had presumably served a long apprenticeship in listening to God. They would only pray in faith when they felt confident that it was God's will that they should pray for healing. We too, before we pray for healing, must ask questions. Is this healing God's next step for this person? Is now the right time to pray? Are we the right people to pray at this time? Much hurt and harm is done when well-meaning people pray out of compassion or hope for healing. In such circumstances the person may be told that they have only to believe to receive. To pray in faith requires an in-touchness with God, a reading of his mind which we find in Jesus. 'I tell you the truth, the Son can do nothing by himself; he can do only what he sees his Father doing, because whatever the Father does the Son also does' (Jn. 5:19). Jesus in his prayer life and his moment by moment in-touchness patterns to us one requirement of the person who would walk in his steps and learn to pray in faith. We too can be so in touch with the Father, listening to him, that we may 'see' what he is doing in a particular situation. Then we can pray accordingly.

Discovering and deploying this method of prayer

The initiation of this ministry of prayer for healing can come by a sudden outpouring of power and authority within a given gathered situation (as in the Acts of the Apostles). We at St Nicholas received a very real step forward when Bishop David Pytches and his wife came to lead our church weekend in January 1984 at Swanwick. We who already believed and ministered in healing suddenly saw the power and authority of Jesus demonstrated in a new way in the Saturday morning sessions. It was an unforgettable experience for the group of nearly 200 of us who had gathered. More usually, development in this ministry arises from ministry gifts exercised by a minority of the congregation. These are gradually recognized as valid and of increasing significance and the ministry of healing within the fellowship develops around these.

For us at St Nicholas the ministry of healing developed slowly over nearly ten years to the holding of regular healing services on Sundays (level three, see my introduction). The move to the willingness to pray openly and expectantly for healing (level four) really dated from that parish weekend. Some nine months later saw a number of our members attending a John Wimber conference. In February 1985 we taught the gathered church as much as we could about this ministry over three Sunday evenings and three Tuesday evenings. On these occasions in-depth teaching was given and each time a prolonged session of praying for one another under supervision was allowed for. Congregations of up to 400 were present at these teach-ins. Scores of people were ministered to on each occasion and we found that our available resources of supervision were acutely stretched.

From that major teach-in many people came forward for teaching and training in this ministry. More went to conferences, and monthly gatherings were held at St Nicholas to teach and train those who wanted to be involved in the ministry. At this time we began to offer the ministry of prayer at each Sunday service. By summer 1986 we had some sixty people who were regularly involved. As we watched over the results of prayer we saw that God was clearly at work, but, as in many ministries where God is at work, enthusiasm can outrun wisdom and experience. Before we got involved in unfortunate experiences it was necessary to expand the teaching, and strengthen oversight. Autumn 1986 saw a ten-week intensive teaching program to fill out the understanding of those ministering. Eighty to a hundred attended and were both encouraged in this ministry and taught the background understanding of personality needs and damage.

At the time of writing our team numbers one hundred, which is divided into four groups under a supervisor. They meet regularly with their supervisor and work as a team offering ministry one service a fortnight. New members are apprenticed to more experienced people and ministry is always in pairs, preferably a man and a woman. In each of these teams there is at least one church elder.

The thrust of this section is to describe how this ministry occurs in church (services). It is basic to our understanding of the ministry that it is at home at street level and is to be exercised from the home and in the house church group as well as the place of work. As in Jesus' day and the early church, it is intended to be a part of everyday life and is not merely therapeutic, but also powerfully evangelistic. On Sundays it would be easy for such a ministry to dominate the services. On occasion it clearly does. On balance the Word and worship are prominent and prayer ministry, although obvious, is in the background.

Before each service up to thirty of us gather for prayer, partly to intercede for the service and to pray for those taking part. The half-hour is divided in two and half of the time is spent in silent prayer, 'listening to God'. During this time we would expect to be reminded of scriptures, receive 'pictures', words of knowledge, prophetic words. These would be shared at the end of the time of silence, noted down, tested and weighed by those leading the service, together with elders. The material would then shape up certain parts of the services, being shared as appropriate, for example, to lead into confession, but more usually to indicate to particular people that we believe God would wish to minister to them at that service.

Care is now taken to ensure the Word is preached sufficiently early on in the service to allow time to respond to the words. In our experience it is the preaching of the Word (20–35 minutes) which produces the focal impact around which would cluster the response, which includes the prayer ministry. At present the sermon will be followed by a brief prayer or bidding leading into absolute silence for personal prayer and reflection lasting up to three or four minutes. At this time those leading the service are attempting to assess under the spirit of God what is the appropriate continuing response. Occasionally we would sense a powerful awareness of the presence of the spirit of God and having identified this would seek to give God the freedom to minister to needs throughout the congregation. More often, following the quiet, we would move into a time of praise and adoration appropriate to the word preached. This would be followed by an invitation to respond to the Word of God and we would share some of those things which we believe God had given us in the time of listening at the beginning of the service. The ministry of prayer would begin in the chancel as the formal part of the service draws to an end. During Holy Communion this prayer ministry would be offered behind the communion table in the chancel during the time of administration of bread and wine.

The ministry offered would be responding to a wide variety of expressed needs: physical healing, emotional healing, need for inner healing, desire to become a Christian, repentance, reconciliation, prayer for close friends or relatives in need, demonization, receiving spiritual gifts, filling with the Holy Spirit and the need of guidance and wisdom. Some of these needs require more than a brief session (of say 10–20 minutes' prayer) and facilities are available for referral at this time. Those referred add to the workload of the pastoral staff. On the other hand much personal, pastoral and counselling work, which would formerly have burdened the staff and pastoral workers, is dealt with by God in these prayer times. The worship and the Word have released the power of God to act and have opened the individual to the power of God. In such situations we find that God is working powerfully and incisively.

It should be stressed that tight and strong leadership of Sunday services is necessary where the congregation numbers between 300 and 500 and at which there are always strangers and visitors. Unusual as such services may sound when described on paper, they have a shape, order and integrity which give them validity and significant impact. Many of our visitors comment on this. They recognize what they describe as reality (an authentic experience of the presence of God). The services are thus also, we believe, powerfully evangelistic.

There follows below part of a summary of how we saw this ministry a year before the time of writing. This is taken from a leaflet used in discussions with other local Anglican churches who are involved in the healing ministry.

An approach to the ministry of healing, St Nicholas' Church, Nottingham

A theological approach
We believe
1. That the healing ministry is the healing of Jesus, one of the fruits of his death on the cross (Isaiah 53) and something which we, his followers, are commissioned to do.
2. That God desires wholeness for his people. This wholeness includes forgiveness of sin and the healing of the body and the emotions (past and present).
3. That alongside a theology of healing must stand a theology of pain; that some suffering is redemptive in the

sense that it is an entering into the pain of the world and as such is an identification with the ongoing sufferings of Christ (see Col. 1) and the suffering which is a part of the package of discipleship since discipleship involves us in working for the extension of Christ's kingdom and will inevitably expose us to fatigue, rejection, loneliness, over-busyness.

4. That healing is a free gift of God, an expression of his love, not a merited bonus.

5. That healing is a mystery; we cannot understand the way it happens nor why some people are healed while others are not.

6. God is sovereign: 'Aslan is not a tame lion' (C.S. Lewis). We must allow him to be God and to exercise his sovereignty by healing some and not others.

7. That God is capable of healing everyone – even raising the dead.

A theoretical approach
We believe

1. That the ministry of healing is a ministry of the Body which therefore takes place in the Body rather than it being a unique 'gifting' of certain individuals (although some individuals clearly are used by God in specific ways, *e.g.* some in the area of physical healing, others in the area of emotional healing, others in the deliverance ministry. Some seem, under God, to become 'specialists' in their field, at least for a limited period.)

2. That, where possible, ministry should be given in teams of at least two (*cf.* the biblical pattern of this) and, where possible, this should be a man and woman team who offer an expression of the mother-love and the father-love of God.

3. That those in the praying team should be accountable to someone who is ultimately responsible to the staff.

4. That follow-up should be offered where appropriate.

5. That regular training should be built into the church's programme to ensure that the help offered is as skilled as possible.

6. That deep reliance on openness to the Holy Spirit of

God, married to an awareness of psychological insights and biblical teaching, make for the best possible kind of ministry.

7. That persons involved in this ministry should have as many people-helping models at their fingertips as possible.

8. That wherever possible we liaise with the helping professions, *e.g.* referring people to GPs, psychiatrists, physiotherapists, osteopaths, where this seems appropriate.

9. That the healing ministry should find its place within the context of the preaching of the Word of God and worship; that the three go together.

10. That the healing ministry should find its full flowering in small group situations, *e.g.* the music group, home fellowships, staff meetings; that it should even spill over to our place of work because it is evangelistic as well as therapeutic.

11. That we should try to prevent pain from arising as well as bringing God's healing to it when it does come. So we anticipate crises and organize activities for engaged couples to prepare them for the adjustment to marriage, seminars for pregnant parents to prepare them for parenthood, marriage fulfilment seminars for married couples to provide an environment where they can deepen their love for one another, and events for the unemployed where they can receive group support.

12. That we should avail ourselves of the gifts of the Spirit in this ministry (wisdom, discernment, the word of knowledge); that people must therefore be trained in the art of listening to God.

Future approach
We believe

1. That God is challenging us at the moment to provide more training for those involved in the prayer ministry whose only qualification for people-helping is that they have attended a John Wimber conference. A training program is to be launched this autumn.

2. That God is challenging us to live biblically: not to become so absorbed in the exciting, up-front, more flam-

boyant ministry of healing that we neglect the house-bound, the elderly, the depressed, the bereaved – those who would find it hard to squeal for help. The training course will therefore include the training of a home visiting team.
3. That we need to strengthen our links with the caring professions in the area so that when we do reach the ceiling of our skills we know where to refer 'hard cases'.
4. That we should look far more carefully at the possibility of apprenticing the newcomer to those who are more experienced – that the network of supervisors should be strengthened.
5. That we owe it to God and people in pain to provide the best help possible, not to be simplistic, triumphalistic or sloppy in our people-helping.
6. That those involved in this ministry should be encouraged to go on learning – never to be allowed to feel that they have arrived.

Response to David Huggett

Philip H. Hacking

In reading David Huggett's contribution and then re-reading my own chapter, I am happily aware of many similarities. Christ Church, Fulwood, in Sheffield is not dissimilar to St Nicholas's in Nottingham except that we are in a more parochial context. Both of us care about the centrality of the message preached and both of us sense the danger of the over-dramatization of commitment, whether in an evangelistic response or in terms of healing. I rejoice that he speaks of the need for strong leadership, which I believe is vital, whatever the pattern of church life and ministry. Although our terminology may differ, clearly we both put stress on counselling. David has made his chapter much more personal to his church than I have mine but we at Christ Church are also busy looking at the structures of our pastoral care, with much more emphasis on the availability of trained and Spirit-filled ministry after a church service, as well as in the continuing life of the church in the community. Of course there are very obvious differences and it is healthy that the church should have a variety of traditions and emphases. We need to learn understanding of each other and the right kind of tolerance. Some of our differences stem from a theological difference of approach but also from the pattern of our church lives. In Fulwood we are set in the midst of a more static community and therefore much of the ministry of caring has a longer-term view than in a city centre community.

There still remain, however, some differences and degrees of unhappiness. I would want to stress that spiritual maturity is more important than counselling skills, and I am fearful of Christians being trained in attitudes to healing which are not biblically based. Reading David's chapter has increased my concern about the stress on inner healing, and I believe we are in danger of dabbling in realms which lie beyond our understanding and applying diagnoses which are not scriptural. David stresses that the elders should be trained in listening to God. I believe that this kind of spiritual leadership asks for much more. I am concerned that my church leaders to whom people should go for counsel should be well versed in the Word of God and very mature in lives of holiness.

I do not honestly believe that people who profess to renounce evil in the Anglican liturgy are talking in terms of the rejection of demonic activity. Nor do I accept David's interpretation of being demonized. I am all the more insistent that we should be concerned about the devil's activity not in such dramatic ways but in his infiltration into every part of our lives through the temptations of the world and the flesh, which are ever his handmaids. It may well be true, as I will comment in my chapter, that in some pioneer situations we are more aware of this kind of demonic activity and therefore the miraculous is more apparent. But I am fearful of the illogical conclusion that somehow we are missing what is happening in our own church life because we do not see these kind of activities to the fore. It is always tempting to emphasize the spectacular and Christians seem to be obsessed by it in these days.

I am not convinced by David's exposition of John 14:12. I believe Pentecost did demonstrate the greater works in the adding of 3,000 to the kingdom at one moment of time. It is not to deny the continuance of signs and wonders but it is to expect the greater manifestation of the truths to which these signs and wonders pointed. I reiterate the comment in my chapter which follows that there is a uniqueness about the ministry of Jesus which I would expect and I do not honestly believe that we are called to be looking for the resurrection of dead people but rather to be proclaiming the eternal life that is ours in Christ, leading to that glorious final resurrection. I would therefore not wish to agree with theological statement number 2 in David's chapter (p.152) that we should expect wholeness which includes healing of the body. It does not seem to me scriptural that we are to expect healing and health at all times. Surely physical death will come to us and God does work through suffering. Therefore I may not expect physical wholeness at all times. To expect this is to see all suffering as a lack of faith or a judgment upon sin in my life. This I believe to be theologically incorrect and spiritually disastrous.

Amongst my other differences of opinion are my instinctive reaction against the belief that anyone may have the spiritual perception to know God's will in individual cases at all times. I see the dangers being worked out in some modern cults which almost make a particular individual so much in tune with God that he becomes infallible and no more needs the direction of God's Word. The Lord may give us an awareness of a particular need by his Spirit working through our mind. But I believe we need a great deal of humility at this level. Nor am I happy about the 'command of faith' idea. We are suffering too much from 'name it, claim it' theology. Ultimately it leads to the prosperity syndrome which I am sure David would deny as much as I. My faith in God's sovereignty leaves me content to trust him to provide the blessings and the health he sees that I need at any given time. We should be glad that the ministry of healing has not been allowed to die; we must be careful that it does not become so much the centre of our thinking that it obscures the greater riches that are ours in Christ.

A ministry easily over-emphasized

Philip H. Hacking

A personal anecdote · It is difficult to get any blueprint for 'ordinary church life' in the New Testament · The New Testament writings do not see the early Christian community as having a healing ministry · Exorcism and the role of the prophet disappear after Acts · The gifts · Prayer for healing is a normal part of the prayer life of the church · Signs and wonders · True gospel ministry will always have healing power and proclaim the defeat of the evil one · Concern for the needs of people · We must beware of a negative reaction to the healing movement and maintain a biblical balance · We mustn't rule out the supernatural but need to recognize that there are other spirits · The importance of testing

This chapter is being written in the context of pastoral life in a normal parish setting, full of the interwoven drama of healing and suffering. I have seen in very dramatic and very ordinary circumstances the rhythm of health and sickness which the Lord allows to his people. It would be possible to give many illustrations of prayer answered in restored physical strength, often through normal medical channels and sometimes beyond normal medical expectations. But it is also being written in the aftermath of the death of a very great Christian friend and churchwarden in my parish. In some ways I could have dedicated this whole chapter to him. His death has already brought life and blessing to a number of people and the service of thanksgiving to celebrate his life was almost like an evangelistic guest service. David was a man who lived with heart trouble and knew the possibility of sudden death, yet he gave his all to the Lord and in life and death brought glory to God. Like the apostle Paul he wanted God to be glorified whether by his life or death (Phil. 1:20). There is no doubt whatever that God had, in his sovereignty, decided to call this good man to himself and nobody ever suggested that this was a moment of failure or lack of faith on the part of anybody, just God in his infinite wisdom and mercy using a life and using a death in his own purposes.

In my pastoral ministry I have seen many movements come and go in regard to the healing ministry, from the days when there was a total non-expectation of anything happening outside the ordinary realm to an almost obsessional fantasy world which makes very many claims – but claims in which many of us find very little substance. There was a time when a deviant movement like Christian Science was there to remind us that there is physical healing which happens without obvious medical care. But now there is a real danger that physical healing is usurping the centrality in many churches and taking the place of the preaching of Christ crucified. Instead of expecting deep-seated miracles of God's Spirit changing lives we become content with something often superficial and always less than central. Salvation in the New Testament speaks of wholeness and therefore we know that God is interested in the physical aspect of our lives, but a basic truth of Christian experience must always be that expressed in Paul's testimony in 2 Corinthians 4:16: 'Though outwardly we are wasting away, yet inwardly we are being renewed day by day'.

It is difficult to find any blueprint for 'ordinary church life' in the New Testament (see 'Starting-point' 25, p. 21). But certainly the epistles are almost devoid of any reference to physical healing as part of the ministry of that church life in its settled state. There are very many references in these epistles to the power of God evidenced in the actual preaching of the gospel and there can be little doubt where the priority ministry is to be found. The numerous exhortations to live holy lives as proof of new

life in Jesus and the numerous commands to spread abroad
the good news are illustrations of this. The apostle Paul
in writing to Corinth in 1 Corinthians 2:4 refers to his
ministry in the city as 'with a demonstration of the Spirit's
power'. You will search in vain in the Acts narrative of
the ministry at Corinth to find any reference to miracles of
healing or casting out of demons. Indeed in 1 Corinthians
1:22–23 Paul contrasts the insatiable desire of the Jews
for signs with his simple proclamation of Christ crucified.
But in that proclamation there is the true power of God
at work. Equally in 1 Thessalonians 1:5 Paul will refer to
his ministry as being 'with power, with the Holy Spirit
and with deep conviction'. Once again a reference back to
that Thessalonian ministry in Acts speaks of very faithful
exposition of Scripture and the effect of it. That is seen in
1 Thessalonians 1:9–10 in a people turned to God from
idols and now serving the living and true God.

It is not surprising therefore that even in the Acts of the
Apostles, when Peter and John had caused a stir by healing
the lame man, the challenge of the authorities was not
that they should cease their healing ministry but that they
should cease preaching in the name of the Lord Jesus (Acts
4:18). It is clear that the power of the Spirit is to be
seen primarily in the effect of a message proclaimed with
conviction. That message by its power could well have a
revolutionary effect on the person, producing that 'inner
healing' of which we hear so much today. Indeed as a side
issue it could well have brought much physical healing in
its train. It is all part of the power of the gospel and that
great word 'salvation'.

Yet it must be conceded that in the narrowest sense of
the term the New Testament writings do not see the early
Christian community as having a healing ministry. Apart
from the significant reference in James to which we shall
return, and an almost incidental reference to healing in
the list of the gifts of the Spirit in 1 Corinthians 12, there
is virtual silence on the theme of physical healing in that
early Christian community beyond the Acts of the
Apostles. It is always dangerous to argue from silence and
it could be that this healing ministry was so much part of

the church life that there was no need for any comment. On the other hand it would be very difficult to adduce that this physical healing ministry was a primary task of the church when there is such a massive silence on the subject.

Certainly there is no remit for a ministry of physical healing in public worship (see question N, p. 22). Even the significant verses in James 5 refer to a personal request to the elders of the church to lay hands on the sick person and it would certainly seem to be within the context of the privacy of the home. Much contemporary excitement over the resurgence of a healing ministry ignores the steady pastoral care of ministers and other Christians in visitation and prayer. Sometimes the spectacular is being sought at the expense of the faithful. Moreover the verses encourage the concept of healing as the pastoral care of the whole church expressed in its leadership. It is probably significant that the sick man is to call for the elders and not for those who have been given particular gifts of healing.

There are no references to exorcism being carried out in the early church outside the gospels and the Acts of the Apostles, with the very clear suggestion that many of the signs and wonders which are evident in the gospels and less obviously in Acts are not perpetuated in the life of the church. The gospel writers see the signs and wonders as primarily an authentication of the unique ministry of our Lord and the early church. St John ends his gospel (20:30–31) by giving us the plan of his writing which is to lead to faith in Christ and to life through his name. The typical signs reported are meant to lead to that end. Where the church has been established and Scripture is fully available it may be that these signs and wonders become less significant. Missionaries in pioneer areas often testify to this pattern. The early days of gospel breakthrough are attested by unusual miracles. Then when the work is well founded these appear to cease, although the miracle of changed lives continues and increases. It is vital to recollect that our Lord's healing ministry was for all who came and was always completely and immediately successful. Never in church history has there ever been anything remotely approaching that kind of ministry and we who believe in the unique person of our Lord should not be surprised.

Within the New Testament local and itinerant ministries overlap and we have some evidence that the role of the prophet in its fullest sense disappears when the New Testament scriptures are available and the authoritative Word of God is known. It is an absolutely vital part of New Testament Christianity that Scripture contains all things necessary to salvation and that we are to bow before its final judgment on all things. Every so-called prophetic word must come under that authority and this is equally relevant in the constantly recurring teaching about the problem of suffering and the ministry of healing. Nowhere does Scripture suggest that God means man always to be physically well. It is not helpful to surmise what our world would have been like had the fall never occurred, whether man would have been immortal and not subject to decay. But since that event human beings, like the rest of creation, groan and travail in pain (Rom. 8:18–23). Only in the new heaven and earth with our resurrected bodies will we be free from pain and physical deterioration. In God's economy the sufferings of this world can become a gateway to a greater understanding of God, hence the dramatic message of the Book of Job. It is not only Paul's thorn in the flesh which denies the oft-repeated untruth that bodily health is always God's will for us. The whole of Scripture sees suffering as part of the divine plan and, until glory and the final defeat of Satan, suffering, sickness and death will always be our portion.

It is not surprising therefore that there is no evidence of any kind of healing missions or groups of people travelling around with a kind of healing circus in the New Testament (see 26, p. 21). There is evidence of travelling evangelists moving into pioneer areas, and the apostle Paul saw that as one of his greatest ministries (Rom. 15:17ff.). This follows from the clear New Testament pattern that evangelism must be the priority: the gospel of eternal life is needed by all, whereas healing in its narrowest physical sense is not that universal a need.

In all this we are in danger of blowing certain texts

out of all proportion. James 5:13–16 is a very significant passage but it must be taken alongside the rest of Scripture, and must of course be undergirded by experience (see 25 and question T, pp. 21–23). If these verses were meant to suggest that all who in faith call for the elders of the church to pray over them will receive full physical healing, it is a serious difficulty that nowhere in the history of the church has this been fully manifested. It is vital therefore to see what are the themes of these verses.

Positively, they remind us of the power of the prayer of faith which may sometimes be seen not in physical healing but in the power to face testing, to accept the will of God, to witness to him in any circumstance, and to turn in repentance and faith to discover the fullness of God's salvation. James is also instructive in his positive stress on community care and long-term pastoral ministry. Often we live in an age of instant remedies and we are therefore impatient with long-term treatment. God's timetable is not ours and much pastoral healing is of the unspectacular, caring kind of infinitely greater demand and worth.

We are encouraged not only to pray *for* people in need but to pray *with* them, and we are also encouraged to leave the initiative with the sick person. Christians must learn to respect the will and desire of the individual made in the image of God. There is a right kind of interdependence in the New Testament within the body of Christ (*cf*. Gal. 6:2). But we are also exhorted to be independent (*cf*. 1 Thes. 4:12). Some in sickness will accept the weakness and learn through it and others will wish for the healing ministry of the church. We must not dictate to believers any more than to God. In practical terms healing groups can pressurize people in a very unhelpful and sometimes quite disastrous way. But it is vital that sick people should be encouraged as the Lord speaks to them to call for the loving, praying care of the people of God with the expectation that in answer to prayer and, where helpful, the external aid of anointing or laying on of hands, God will move in and do something new. This passage seems supremely to rebuke the common attitude of apathy in the face of suffering. Prayer will anticipate God moving in action. No situation is beyond the control of our God; his arm is not shortened (Is. 59:1).

It is also important in the paragraph in James to notice that there is reference to the forgiveness of sins where these are confessed. The Book of Common Prayer laid great stress on that ministry in the visitation of the sick and we do well not to forget that there are worse ailments than to be physically ill. Our Lord could say to a man who had been paralysed for thirty-eight years and was now well that he should sin no more, lest a worse thing happened to him. It is possible to be so obsessed with the desire for physical well-being that we forget to call people to prepare to meet their God. After all, whatever healing we may receive, one day we die and meet our Maker. Unless we prepare people for that certainty we fail in our ministry.

The continuance of gifts within the church is always a debatable issue (see question M, p. 22). In some ways it would be very tidy to see these signs and wonders as a unique aspect of our Lord's ministry and the immediately post-Pentecost days. Most theologians now would question whether that kind of dispensationalism is actually truly biblical. But there seems to be no obvious link between these signs and the ongoing healing ministry of the settled church. Where gifts *are* being exercised it is important that they should be recognized by the church; much harm is done when people arrogate power to themselves. Self-deception is a constant danger. We must take the body of Christ seriously and look to the wise counsel of others in discovering our gifts and using our opportunities. It is a matter of great concern that we live in an age when people are being encouraged to minister to one another without any awareness of background and training in particular skills. I would never share my deepest concerns with a total stranger, however spiritually minded he may claim to be. I would need to have confidence in the maturity of someone to whom I went for counsel, and that must ever be so. Christian counsellors need to be trained as much as evangelists need training. This is particularly vital in areas of so-called inner healing where great harm can and often has been done.

Praying for healing is a very significant part of church life and ministry, but I believe it to be wisest within the context of the whole prayer life of the church. I have reservations about healing prayer groups, because I see it as a more balanced pattern of intercession to be praying not just for a rather restrictive healing but within the context of the whole evangelistic ministry and pastoral care of the church. There is ever the danger of wrong expectations where healing services are held, or where healing is offered at the communion service. Here it can easily place a greater emphasis on physical healing than on the breaking of bread and the pouring of wine, which is the heart of the communion service; it also can elevate the communion service into a special category which in a sense it does not have. Such services seem to conflict with our Lord's constant desire to keep the healing of people away from the spectacular. Time and again he asked them not to tell others (*e.g.* Mk. 1:34, 44; 5:43). In no way did he wish his healing ministry to be a peep show, and public services of healing very quickly degenerate to that level. Our Lord, far from being excited about the signs and wonders ministry, rejects the Pharisees' desire for a special sign, and laments in John 4:48, 'Unless you people see miraculous signs and wonders, you will never believe'. Another problem of the public healing service is that things have to happen quickly while often the problems are deep-seated and long-term.

Where signs and wonders are spoken of in the New Testament, they are linked with the preaching of the gospel and there can be no doubt where the priority lies (see question C, p. 19). So Paul in Romans 10 speaks of faith coming by hearing and hearing by the Word of God. Yet there are groups who now want to insist that the preaching of the gospel is no longer necessary because the signs and wonders do the work instead of the gospel preacher. It is hard to see this as anything other than a deviation from the New Testament norm. This is particularly dangerous when the signs and wonders degenerate from physical healing to the more unusual manifestations such as the experience called 'being slain in the Spirit' which has no biblical background and whose historical precedents are dubious. Occasionally precedents for this experience are sought in the rare Old Testament action of certain of the prophets as the Lord brought his word to them. But even then they were not called to be mindless. In Numbers 22:31 Balaam fell down but his eyes were open and his mind was being used to hear God's word and to get to know him better. We are never encouraged to anaesthetize our minds in order that we might hear the word of the Lord. He speaks through our minds. There is no similarity between these moments in the Old Testament and the mass emotion which can be encouraged by modern phenomena. The falling down on the face before Jesus in response to his miracles or on the transfiguration mount or in heaven (Lk. 5:8; Mt. 17:6; Rev. 1:17) are far removed from the modern experience of being 'slain in the Spirit'. Days of revival may have had similarities to this but on such occasions the note seems to have been one of repentance and remorse rather than engendered excitement. All too often such spectacular events take the public eye. Not only is there no biblical precedent but we move into very dangerous realms and may be in touch with forces which do not come at all from the Lord. In the New Testament the supreme wonder is that of changed lives and changed communities. Where these are evident the lesser signs and wonders become almost insignificant.

The Christian who believes in the sovereignty of God as paramount will accept that this sovereignty operates in matters of physical healing (see question P, p. 22). There is some evidence that the apostles seemed to be aware that a particular person was ready to be healed and there is no indication that this kind of sensitivity has died. But we have no ability to assume that we know whether or when or how God chooses to heal. Some healing miracles can be just the normal spontaneous remission which is known by the medical profession. Medical science has many parallels which claim no religious origin. We are unwise to draw lines and make dogmatic statements which cannot be proved. The reason why the walls of Jericho fell was of no significance to Joshua; he just rejoiced that in the providence of God they fell at precisely the right moment. A belief in the sovereignty of God will lead to a great deal of prayer and care. It will of course call for Christians to be ready to respond to the invitation to pray with a person in need, and where that person wishes to lay on hands or to anoint with oil. Such a belief will make Christians absolutely honest in their own testimony and wise to observe over a long period before great statements are made. It would be helpful in every way that miracles of healing should have careful medical assessment. The Christian church gains nothing by half-truths. Our Lord sent the cleansed lepers back to the priests as a demonstration of the reality of their healing (Lk. 17:11–19). Because we live in a world obsessed with physical health the church needs to be careful not to be drawn into the spirit of the age.

Some of this obsession goes alongside the very dangerous teaching that promises prosperity to all those who believe and follow the Lord. We need to differentiate between certain Old Testament promises of national prosperity in the land of Canaan for an obedient people (*e.g.* Dt. 8:1–11) and the false concept that in serving our Lord we may expect to prosper in this world's currency. In fact our Lord demands that we sacrifice in his cause and frequently he underlines the dangers and snare of riches. We are called in the New Testament not to give in order that we might get but exactly the reverse (*cf.* Eph. 4:28). We receive so that we can give, expecting nothing in return. In the light of this unbiblical teaching on prosperity, to be unemployed or to be sick is to demonstrate that you are out of tune with God's will. This denies the teaching of Paul, especially in 2 Corinthians, and goes against the experience of Christians in every age. Of course Scripture teaches that God is no man's debtor and there is a true prosperity in following him. But this is quite different from worldly success, just as true health is more vital than physical healing. Ultimately the priority must be the eternal salvation of men and women. It was for this that Jesus died, not for our physical well-being; very quickly the cross will cease to be central if physical healing becomes the obsessive concern of the church. The gospels clearly portray Jesus as moving towards Calvary as the climax of his ministry, not a tragic end but a glorious dénouement. He could cry 'finished' from the cross (Jn. 19:30). This triumphant cry is only meaningful when we think in terms of God dealing once for all with man's most acute problem, sin. The task of healing was quite unfinished. Jesus came primarily not to heal but to save and the pattern of his servant ministry in Mark 10:43–45 is meant to be ours. We may not save but we may preach that saving message, and in so doing serve our fellow men most effectively. It is a simple truth, but one often forgotten, that however much we may be healed death will come. But the miracle of eternal life has effects for all time.

In all the discussion of healing in the life of the church, the word itself has become an omnibus expression, and one then often devalued of meaning. In this way dishonesty and other dangers threaten (see question R, p. 22). Inner healing may be a meaningful term where it speaks about the peace of God brought to bear through the gospel, or an end to bitterness because of ills in the past. I recollect a member of one of my congregations who was conscious of God's touch of healing in a particular service and expected that it would mean that she would be out of her wheelchair and walking. In fact she remained in her wheelchair but found that the bitterness and rebellion had gone and she now had a deep desire to speak of the Lord as well as a great peace of heart. In a wonderful way the miracle of that life was a proclamation from a wheelchair of the grace and love of God which in the long term was a more effective demonstration of God's power than if she had been freed to walk. That may well be what is meant by inner healing, which may again speak of a mind and conscience cleansed through the message of the cross. The ministry of the gospel will always bring that kind of inner healing.

But there are many dangers in the technique which seems to bring inner healing and will often use methodology and language from fundamentally dubious sources. It is dangerous to absorb the terminology of eastern mystic cults or spiritist writings. The New Testament does not use this kind of language. We have no biblical precedent to take people back to their birth experience or to their pre-birth experience or, as sometimes happens now, to the sins of their forefathers. To do all this is dangerous and it denies the efficacy of the message of the cross. Since my sins have been washed away through the blood of Christ there is no need to keep on bringing out the soiled garments to find peace. All this can be tied up with an unbiblical view of man, with a lessening of the message of repentance and the assurance of forgiveness. My sins are all forgotten as well as forgiven in the new covenant (Je. 31:34). Paul speaks of a bond cancelled, of our indictment nailed to the cross (Col. 2:14). The constant proclamation of this message of forgiveness brings that true inner peace to the penitent saved sinner. Not least we must beware of any teaching which denies the true and deep ministry of suffering which is intrinsic to New Testament theology. In 2 Corinthians 1:3–11 Paul can rejoice at the positive nature of suffering, as throwing a person on the resources of God and giving that person such an experience of God's comfort as will spill over in blessing to others.

It is not possible to differentiate between suffering in a physical sense and suffering which comes from persecution. Paul writes in 2 Corinthians 12 about asking for the thorn in his flesh to be taken away three times but discovering God's answer that his strength was made perfect in weakness. We have no idea what was the actual thorn in the flesh, and probably scriptural vagueness is important at this point. But it does speak quite clearly of a deep experience of God's grace. It is that in which Paul will boast rather than in the visions which he had especially been given and which were personal to him. Out of his experience of suffering and comfort in suffering he was able to bring comfort and help to others. The whole of 2 Corinthians breathes that same messge; it is a vital book for the church today. In 2 Corinthians 10:3–4 we are reminded that Christian weapons are spiritual and not worldly. The real power of the gospel is often to be seen in the weakness and suffering of the church. There may be power evangelism but there is also weakness evangelism and often the church's power seems to the world to be weakness. In some deep paradoxes in 2 Corinthians 6:9–10 Paul can speak of himself as 'known, yet regarded as unknown; dying, and yet we live on; beaten, and yet not killed; sorrowful, yet always rejoicing; poor, yet making many rich; having nothing, and yet possessing everything'. This is the constant message of the apostle. We triumph not with worldly weapons of success but with the message of the cross, which to man always seems folly and weakness. The message that came to the early Christian emperor, 'in this sign conquer', should ever be at the heart of our confidence. Jesus was tempted in the wilderness to bypass the cross and use his power in spectacular ways to draw the crowds. He rejected such a signs and wonders mentality as he saw the temptation as satanic. Our enemy has not lost his subtlety. We must beware of any shortcuts to success in church life.

True gospel ministry will always have healing power and proclaim the defeat of the evil one. There will be extreme cases of demon possession where there will need to be extreme measures (see question S, p. 22). The pattern of the gospels will probably be repeated in genuine demon possession. There will be primarily a violent reaction to the name of Jesus, often physically expressed. Exorcism did not die with the early church but casting out non-existent demons can make the last state of the person worse than the first. As in the ministry of physical healing this will need extreme care and sensitivity. There is a strange kind of fascination with evil and demons and some in seeking demons behind every problem are in danger of playing the devil's game for him. Equally, to expect to find victory by the casting out of dubious demons is to want to have a shortcut to holiness. The Bible insists on discipline, on much prayer, on walking with the Lord, on cutting out that which is unhelpful in our lives. The way to holiness in the New Testament is punctuated by commands to walk, wrestle, pray, repent, consecrate, put off, put on. Our Lord could be most challenging in his demands (*cf*. Mt. 5:29–30). In the analogy in those verses the references to bodily suffering are no doubt metaphorical but they underline that to Jesus sin is always a greater evil than suffering. We have a part to play and Satan is more subtle than to work always or even mostly through demon possession. The New Testament records no hierarchy of demons. We must treat Satan very seriously and we must not be ignorant of his devices. Demon possession is probably very rare indeed in our context. The influence of Satan in people's lives is constant. Our victory over him comes primarily through prayer and study and daily discipline.

James 5 is often the beginning and ending of discussion of healing in church life because it is almost unique (see question T, pp. 22–23). It therefore makes sense to end with it. With all the disagreements, this passage of Scripture clearly reminds us that there is a healing ministry in the church, and indicates its dimensions. It assumes that a sick person will normally call for this ministry and expect it to be readily available. Often we have failed to provide in this way. This ministry can be very demanding and far from spectacular. It calls us to prayer and the steadiness of faithful prayer. I believe some of the greatest healing agents I have known have been faithful servants who have gone on praying for and with sick people, not claiming great results but being agents of God's blessing and activity. Of those we need infinitely more.

We are also reminded that there should be a corporate concern for people in need and that the church as a body should take seriously its relationship with every limb in the body. 1 Corinthians 12:26 speaks of all the body suffering with the one limb. Such a relationship can transform suffering and make it a fruitful experience for the whole church. In my pastoral ministry time and again I have discovered the church being brought together in a new way because of some suffering within the family, either of sickness or bereavement. We would have been the poorer without that experience together. In many churches the sick person would have no confidence to call for the elders of the church and we need to have church fellowships where that relationship becomes alive and obviously available. It also means that church elders or leaders should be spiritually mature men and women, able to deal with this sensitive area of need. We need to look at the pastoral care of our church family and be sure that it is for all and not just for the select few. We need to look at our church fellowship meetings and see how they can become more like this particular paragraph in James 5 where there can be mutual sharing and caring, not in a forced way and without becoming agents of church gossip. But they can be places where to pray for one another and to share needs and to lay hands on one another would be quite natural within the safeguards of the total church fellowship.

These verses remind us that there is a value in praying with someone and that physical contact has a place. To pray for people is vital; to pray with them is often a very important extra. However we interpret the phrases about the Lord raising the sick man and bringing healing, we are reminded that only the Lord can do it and only the Lord can bring forgiveness and salvation which are the prime needs of every person. In our Lord's ministry the raising up of the paralysed man was evidence of a greater miracle of God's forgiveness being available to him. The sign has a real place but the reality of which it is a sign is the greater. Only that can make sense ultimately of the promise of Jesus in John 14:12 and its reference to 'greater works than these'. Healing may be a temporary sign of God's favour, though sometimes Christians will actually learn to rejoice that they are counted worthy to suffer. Salvation will be the eternal sign of God's favour and grace. It is not without significance that this very practical letter of James ends on the note of the power of prayer and the great ministry of bringing a sinner back from the error of his ways and saving his soul from death. It will be a mark of wisdom in the local church fellowship that nothing will deflect us from the ultimate goal of our ministry. We shall not neglect the temporal and the physical but we shall certainly not let them obscure the eternal and the spiritual.

In the light of some modern mass movements on this subject of healing which dominate the Christian media by their very nature, we are wise not to be driven to over-react. Some are tempted to climb on every bandwagon and to rush off after every novelty in the manner of the Athenians who are condemned in the Acts of the Apostles. Others of us seek to keep our heads and maintain a biblical balance. We must be aware of the danger of an unduly negative reaction. All of us must expect God to be God and to be at work amongst us. We must never rule out the supernatural but equally we are called not to be naïve in the world and to imagine that everything that smacks of the supernatural has come from our heavenly Father. There are other spirits at work and we need the constant reminder of the New Testament to test the spirits. Every person engaged in Christian work would be wise to remember the balance at the end of Paul's first letter to the Thessalonians (5:19–22): 'Do not put out the Spirit's fire; do not treat prophecies with contempt. Test everything. Hold on to the good. Avoid every kind of evil.'

Response to Philp H. Hacking

David Huggett

I can hear David Watson saying, memorably, 'The answer to misuse is not disuse but right use'. This chapter seems to encourage us too far in the direction of disuse of the ministry of healing.

'Jesus came primarily not to heal but to save', we are told. Is this true? Can we divide the two? We seem to hear that the spirit is more important than the body (*cf.* use of 2 Cor. 4:16); spiritual changes are seen as 'deep-seated miracles', physical healing merely 'superficial'. The Bible treats man as a unity. Jesus came to seek and to 'save' (Mt. 18:11). This word for 'save' (*sozo*) is used by the angels (Mt. 1:21). Jesus uses this word to describe, separately, healing and forgiveness. So do the New Testament writers. Had it been necessary to distinguish between healing and forgiveness in his saving work there are good alternative words for healing in New Testament use. We are left in no doubt that 'Jesus saves' includes both healing and forgiveness. They are indissolubly linked. Together they flow from Calvary (*e.g.* Is. 53:5). Truly we rejoice, for 'ransomed, healed, restored, forgiven, Who like me his praise should sing?'.

To say that 'nowhere does the scripture suggest that God means man always to be physically well' also diminishes the importance of healing. But Jesus was fully human, never sick, and he is our perfect pattern as much in holiness and grace as in health and well-being. That in neither do we measure up to our pattern does not invalidate God's will that we should be like him.

'It is vital to recollect that our Lord's healing ministry was for all who came and was always completely and immediately successful.' This serves to detach his ministry from ours, but here too he is our pattern. He is not so far removed as to be an inappropriate model, for the above assertion is too stark. A partial and progressive pattern is recorded in Mark 8:22ff. Frequently Jesus escaped from those who were seeking to come to him (*e.g.* Mk. 1:36; Lk. 5:15f.). He healed only one of the many at the Bethesda Pool, slipping away through the crowd before he could be waylaid by others (Jn. 5:3,13). He must often have passed the man at the Gate Beautiful, hearing his piteous cry, but that cry was not to be answered yet. God had other plans for that man. Jesus appears saddened and surprised by his ineffectiveness in Matthew 13:58.

We are told that the true locus of the power of God today is to be seen in preaching. Thus the story of Acts 3 and 4 demonstrates 'that the power of the Spirit is to be seen primarily in the effect of the message proclaimed'. Is this so? In Acts 3:6 Peter *speaks* to the man to be healed *in the name of Jesus*. The authorities question, 'By what power or what name did you do this?' (4:7). Peter replies that it was *in the name of Jesus* (4:10) that he spoke to this man; that's how he was healed. The authorities ask what they are going to do to stop the apostles doing this sort of thing (4:16f.). 'Warn these men to *speak* no longer to anyone *in this name*'. The authorities' concern was not to stop them preaching but rather the speaking of authoritative words of healing.

Two things underline this interpretation. First, only once in Acts 3 and 4 is the ministry called 'preaching' (4:2). Normally it is 'speaking' or 'speaking the word'. Second, the prayer of the church (4:23ff.) is not that they should preach boldly, but that they should 'speak your word with great boldness' (verse 29; *cf.* verse 31). This is not splitting hairs. There is no full-stop between verse 29 and verse 30 (see AV not NIV). Thus verse 30 amplifies 'speak your word'. (Careful examination of the Greek grammar here is instructive.) They pray in effect to continue boldly to *speak in the name of Jesus* in the manner of Acts 3:6. This is the way which ushers in healing, signs and wonders, and is followed (importantly) with the sharing of the truth. Preaching answers the questions raised by the healings and other signs, but I submit that these chapters are all about the power of the Spirit seen in healing and the like, and not primarily about the power of the Spirit in preaching.

Finally, I wonder if it is helpful in dealing with the demonic to use emotive terms like exorcism and demon possession. The first is not a biblical word (except in Acts 19:13). The second is sometimes used to translate and represent a biblical word or condition which would be more accurately represented by 'demonization'. Demonization helpfully speaks of the New Testament spectrum of demonic involvement, much of which falls far short of possession. Demonization is still a major problem: as I write I have just returned from ministry in France, where there is one spiritual medium for every 120 people and occultism is a way of life. Shortly I return to Malaysia and Singapore for ministry. From there and from the many Chinese in our congregation I have learnt the importance of teaching and putting into practice spiritual warfare and ministry to the demonized. A new generation grows up around whom occult practice and involvement is prevalent. We are fighting a well-organized and numerous body of demonic spirits and angels (Eph. 6:11ff.; Rev. 12:9) who are strategically deployed. Thank God that in his Name we have the victory.

Philip Hacking is right in commenting adversely about the unhealthy preoccupation of some fellowships in this area. But once again the answer to abuse is not disuse but right use. In this area, as in many others, we need to take a fresh close look at Scripture, that we may learn how to be fully equipped to minister in the 1990s.

Part 4:
Conclusion: analysing the issues

John Goldingay

A number of areas of agreement emerge from the above pages: that God does heal, that he uses medical and non-medical, ordinary and extraordinary methods, that in some sense healing is an appropriate concern of the church. My aim in these final pages is to analyse the areas of disagreement which also emerge or underlie the chapters.

1. What are the implications of gospel references to illness and healing?
Much ministry of healing implicitly bases itself on what Jesus did, on what he commissioned his immediate disciples to do, and on what the apostles in Acts did, though it does not always make explicit the basis on which we take up the same kind of ministry. What indication does the New Testament give that the church is expected to continue the kind of spectacular healing ministry undertaken by Jesus himself, by his disciples during his lifetime, and by the apostles?

In the discussion in this book, four passages have surfaced as possible indications of this. Mark 16:17–18 must surely be reckoned out of court, since Mark 16:9–20 does not seem to belong to the original Gospel; it is missing from 'the most reliable early manuscripts' (NIV).

We can hardly use it to establish a point not made else-where in undisputed parts of Scripture. John 14:12 promises that the disciples will do greater works than Jesus, but exegetes do not take this to denote the performing of miraculous signs and wonders greater than Jesus's (which would in any case prove too much: see Peter May, p. 41). Are advocates of the 'signs and wonders' approach misinterpreting Scripture in the light of their experience, or are exegetes misinterpreting Scripture in the light of their (lack of) experience (see 4 below)? The latter make an impressive point when they suggest that John 14:12 needs to be understood in the light of John 5:20–21, where the 'greater works' is the giving of new spiritual life to people; this does seem the natural understanding of John 14:12 also. According to John 20:21 we are sent as Jesus was, but again this cannot simply be assumed to include a healing ministry like Jesus's (Peter May, p. 40). According to Matthew 28:16–20, the disciples are to teach people everything Jesus has commanded them, but again this proves too much: there are things Jesus commanded the disciples to do which they do not have to tell others to *do*, even though they do tell them about them (Mt. 10:5; 16:20; 26:18).

There remains, then, a worrying absence of mandate from the New Testament for undertaking the kind of healing ministry that Jesus, his immediate disciples, and the apostles did.

2. What are the implications of references to illness and healing in the epistles?

The epistles include a number of references to illness and few references to healing ministry (see *e.g.* Philip Hacking, pp. 161–162). But the latter seem enough to me to establish that healing is a natural part of the church's ministry, a more natural part than it has often been. They also establish, however, that there is nothing odd about the fact that people often do not get healed. Illness, like sin, continues to be part of life in this age.

If we bracket the gospels and Acts because of the consideration just noted, what kind of mandate for what kind of healing ministry do the epistles give us? 1 Corinthians 12 looks like encouragement towards *some* expectation of miracle *sometimes*, even if we accept that the miraculous will never be the norm in this age. And James 5 looks like an encouragement to take prayer for healing as a norm whether or not the leaders of the church believe they have gifts in this area.

3. *What is actually happening?*

Roger Cowley declares that 'for substantial numbers [of 'miracles'] reliable documentation is available' (p. 90); Tony Dale relates a number of experiences from his own and other people's lives. Peter May questions the interpretation of these. Tony Dale warns us against scepticism, Peter May against gullibility. I myself would like to believe that lots of miracles are happening, but like Peter May find hard evidence difficult to come by. The clear miracles happen somewhere else; the things that happen when I am there are more psychosomatic (though no less real and worthwhile for that) and/or rather trivial and not very like the kind of thing related in the gospels and Acts. I am a bit puzzled by the difficulty in establishing how much is happening that is medically inexplicable. This looks like a matter of empirical facts on which it ought to be possible to reach agreement!

4. *What is the significance of what is going on?*

A number of contributors give considerable space to relating their own and other people's experiences, mostly of healing being given, sometimes of it being withheld. What is the significance of this material? What is the relationship between what we learn from what is happening today and what we learn from Scripture? Roger Cowley (p. 96) affirms the primacy of biblical teaching over experience. David Huggett (p. 139), however, questions whether we need explicit validation from Jesus for patterning our ministry on his, and follows it with reference to his own experience which apparently provides the validation for his approach. But can it do so? How does this approach differ from the one taken by the Moonies, with their stress on experience? Thus evangelicals have traditionally maintained that we move from Scripture to experience. On the other hand, David Huggett notes that people who use Scripture to dispute his approach may have other more covert (experiential!) reasons for doing so. So even if we profess to believe that it is right theologically to move from Scripture to experience, in practice our understanding of Scripture is influenced by our experience. When we recognize that, we can start safeguarding against the negative aspects to it; we are more likely to be in trouble if we do not allow for that possibility and fail to become self-critical regarding our relationship with Scripture. Experience is not self-interpreting. An account of personal experiences can become the basis for reliable theological reflection only when these experiences are set in the light of Scripture. Interpreting Scripture in the light of experience is a journey round a vicious circle. We need to be wary of an unreflective matching of (alleged) experiences with scriptural texts superficially read. This is a danger for both 'sides' in this argument.

5. How significant is the body?
David Huggett stresses the interweaving of body and mind and thus of emotional and spiritual problems and physical illness (pp. 145–146). This rather contrasts with Peter May's opening treatment of the significance of bodily health. Does the latter underplay the body's significance in Scripture? Scripture sees human beings as a psycho-physical whole, and it is the whole person who is made in God's image. The idea of an image suggests something material and visible – an immaterial, invisible image sounds a contradiction in terms. Christologically it is important that the image of God lies in humanity's full psycho-physical nature: it is this that made the incarnation possible, indeed 'natural'. Shalom, which Peter May emphasizes, is a notion that applies to the material at least as much as the realm of the spirit, and resurrection involves the whole psycho-physical person. We do not believe in John Brown's body lying a-moulding in the grave while his soul goes marching on: his soul feels

distinctly incomplete without his body and would like to have it back again, renewed, please – as 2 Corinthians 5 indicates.

Material and spiritual belong together in Scripture. If the material affects the spiritual (Peter May, p. 36), is the opposite not also true? If we are put right with God and are in this sense spiritually whole, it would be odd if that never had an effect on the rest of our persons. Sometimes I overwork because I am seeking justification by works, and I get backache or some other psychosomatic illness; getting things right between me and God and getting things right between me and my body may interact.

On the other hand, it does not seem to be the case that the more mature we are spiritually, the fitter we are physically. God does not bring his most mature saints to him by making it possible for them to evade death, but by taking them through death and making it the way to resurrection. Similarly he takes them through aging and suffering, not as something in tension with spiritual maturity and trust in him, but as a means to it. A theology of 'signs and wonders' needs to be clear what it is saying theologically about the realities of suffering and dying among the people of God, which will continue to be realities on a vast scale as long as we belong to this age (won't they?) (*cf.* Bill Lees, response p. 107).

6. What is the relationship between the cross and healing? Peter May notes correctly that Matthew 8:17 is not about the death of Christ, but the actual idea that the atonement included dealing with illness does not seem to me incoherent, though to speak of Christ atoning for our sicknesses may be too shorthand a way to put it. My personal experience of illness may not result from my personal sin (*cf.* Job and Jn. 9). Nevertheless the presence of illness in general in the world results from evil in the world, which itself results from the presence of sin in the world. If Christ deals in principle with sin and evil, then, he thereby deals in principle with illness. Insofar as all illness results from the presence of evil in the world, all healing, like all forgiveness, is a fruit of his death, which produces this gracious fruit before his time as well as after it. It is in keeping with this that bodily resurrection (his and ours) is, among other things, a sign that his work of atonement has been effective: the spiritual work 'naturally' has a physical outward expression. In Christ God has won the victory over evil. But resurrection belongs to the End. That victory is not yet completely effective in this age. And because the illness (and the death) of believers issue as much from the general presence of evil in the world as from our personal sin, it is also quite 'natural' that believers still experience illness and death.

7. *Prayer and knowledge of God's will*

The approach to healing ministry advocated by David Huggett emphasizes discovering whether it is God's will to heal someone, and then praying in faith for him to do so. I accept that God does sometimes reveal to us what he wants to give us, and that listening to God is an important aspect of prayer. If we know what God is going to do, we can indeed pray expectantly. Nevertheless I have two questions about this emphasis. First, is this what references to 'praying according to God's will' (1 Jn. 5:14) mean? I would have thought they more likely refer to praying for the *kind* of thing God is likely to grant (in the light of what he has done for us and the way he has revealed himself to us in Christ), such as people's conversion – or their healing! Which leads me to the second question. Whether or not we want to talk about prayer altering God's mind, it surely does mean asking God to do things he would not otherwise do. The prayers of Abraham, Moses, and Jesus suggest that we discover what God wants to give us partly by asking for things and seeing whether he grants them. Prayer thus involves risking the answer 'no'. It would be a shame not to pray because we lacked an assurance that God wanted to grant this particular thing: better to risk a prayer that God does not grant than to miss something he might grant (Jas. 4:2b)!

About the contributors

John Goldingay is Principal of St John's College, Nottingham. He has recently completed writing a major commentary on Daniel.

Roger Cowley, an eminent scholar in Ethiopian studies, was a missionary teacher in Ethiopia, before joining the staff of Oak Hill College, London, and working in a parish in Chorleywood. After contributing to this book leukemia was diagnosed, and he died shortly afterwards.

Tony Dale, a medical doctor, pioneered the Tower Hamlets Christian Fellowship before becoming involved full-time with Caring Professions Concern, which he heads. The expansion of this work has led to Tony and his family moving to the United States.

Philip Hacking, Chairman of the Keswick Convention, is an Anglican Vicar in a busy parish church on the outskirts of Sheffield. He has conducted university missions in the UK, and preached in Australia, Korea, Japan, Jamaica, India, Barbados and, often, in Nigeria.

David Huggett did scientific research and worked in aeronautics before training for the ministry. For fifteen years he has been Vicar of St Nicholas' church in the city centre of Nottingham. He and his wife Joyce, an IVP author, have a world-wide teaching and prayer ministry.

Bill Lees, a doctor in Reading, was a missionary in East Malaysia. There he provided a medical service, his wife Shirley translated the New Testament, and together they shared in church-planting and teaching. Their experiences are captured in their book *Is it sacrifice?: Experiencing mission and revival in Borneo* (IVP).

Peter May, a GP in Southampton, is a former UCCF Travelling Secretary. Married with four children, he is a member of the General Synod of the Church of England and chairs the Southampton School of Christian Studies. Peter is particularly interested in evangelism and apologetics. This concern, together with the sobering experience of once being diagnosed as having cancer, lies behind his interest in the theme of this book.

Oliver R. Barclay, the editor of the When Christians Disagree series, was formerly General Secretary of the Universities and Colleges Christian Fellowship. He is the author of *Developing a Christian mind* (IVP).

Index of biblical references

All verse groupings are indexed separately. References in **bold type** *are to whole chapters rather than individual verses.*

Genesis
1 *56*
1:26 *29*
1:28 *17*
2 *56*
3 *56, 146*
50:20 *43*

Exodus
4:9 *87*
11:10 *87*
15:26 *58f.*

Numbers
22:31 *167*

Deuteronomy
6:8 *87*
8:1–11 *168*
34:7 *60*

Joshua
1:2–3 *109f.*
5:12 *81*
10 *109*

Judges
7:7, 9 *109*

1 Samuel
16:14 *59*

2 Kings
7:6–7 *109*
20:1–7 *20*

2 Chronicles
16:12 *20*

Job
1:8 *43*
17:13–15 *43*

Psalms
73:25 *12*
103:3–5 *63*
122 *28*
126 *13*

Isaiah
9:6 *28*
30:21 *118*
53 *17, 68, 152*
53:4–5 *108, 131*
53:4f. *38f.*
53:5 *175*
53:10 *57*
57:15, 18–21 *28*
59:1 *165*

Jeremiah
31:34 *170*

Ezekiel
34:4 *72*

Joel
2:30 *87*

Matthew
1:21 *175*
4:23–24 *58*
5:29–30 *172*
6:10 *52*
6:11 *109*
7:22 *93*
8:2 *58*
8:17 *17, 38, 68, 131, 183*
8:27 *138*
9:6, 8 *138*
10:5 *180*
10:8 *39*
11:12 *47*
12:39–40 *40*
13:58 *17, 176*

16:16 *113*
16:20 *180*
17:6 *167*
18:11 *175*
21:21f. *148*
24:24 *87*
26:18 *180*
26:28 *39*
28:16–20 *180*
28:18–20 *40, 138f.*

Mark
1:28, 33 *41*
1:34, 44 *166*
1:36 *176*
1:37–38 *41f.*
1:40–45 *42*
1:41 *92*
2 *20*
2:1–12 *17*
2:5 *17, 43*
2:10 *138*
2:11 *43*
2:12 *79*
5:27–29 *92*
5:34 *17*
5:43 *166*
6:13 *101*
7 *67*
8:22ff. *176*
8:23 *101*
9:24 *58*
10:25 *17*
10:43–45 *169*
13:22 *93*
16 *17*
16:9–20 *179*
16:17–18 *40, 179*

Luke
4:14–21 *138*
4:32 *138*
4:36 *138*

General index

Many topics recur throughout the book and so have been indexed only where they are key concepts in the argument. The Index of biblical references should be used in conjunction with this index: e.g. when looking for information on the prayer of faith, references to James 5:13–16 should also be consulted.